Eating an Elephant

Write Your Life One Bite at a Time

Also by Patricia Charpentier

Bringing Your Ancestors to Life

Focus on Writing—Book 1: Get Started Writing Your Life Story

Focus on Writing—Book 2: I Remember

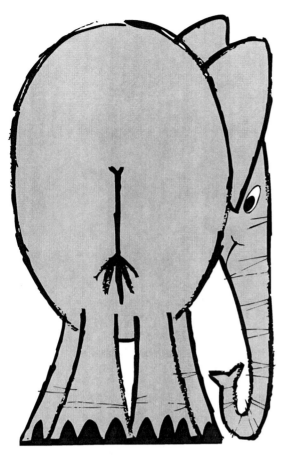

Eating an Elephant

Write your life

One Bite at a Time

Patricia Charpentier

LifeStory Publishing
Orlando, Florida

Eating an Elephant . . .
Write Your Life One Bite at a Time

Patricia Charpentier

LifeStory Publishing
P. O. Box 541527
Orlando, FL 32854

Library of Congress Control Number: 2011911297

ISBN-13: 978-0-9832382-3-2
ISBN-10: 0-9832382-3-5

Printed in the United States of America

Book design by Erin L. Matherne

First Edition: August 2011
10 9 8 7 6 5 4 3 2 1

All grammatical and typographical errors have been put in this book for your enjoyment in finding them.

For Bob, my partner in life . . .

Acknowledgments

For Liam Gillen, who first suggested I write a book—sorry for saying you were crazy,

For Beth Traynor, who believed everything was possible when I didn't,

For Connie Bristow, Denise Fisher and Jennifer Berry, for being the sisters I never had,

For Beverly Bailey, who lovingly put every word in this book to the test,

For my parents, who gave me the culture found on these pages and challenged me to write when I was fourteen,

For Ron Allbee, who was my client, now my mentor and friend,

For Elaine Person, who gave me a great read and rooted out all my favorite words, like *just,*

For the students of Writing Your Life, who bring life to my ideas and share their stories with me,

For Jennifer Paster, Mary Dell Mattingly, Marc Gould, Carole Mayback and all those I'm not able to name here, who offered encouraging words just when I needed them most,

For Ann Clement and Amy Cameron O'Rourke, entrepreneurs teaching me how to be one,

For Wildacres Retreat, who provided a cabin atop a North Carolina mountain to begin writing this book,

For Rick Houle, who provided the perfect getaway to finish writing this book,

For Dr. Lezlie Laws, who rekindled the writing spark and showed me the kind of teacher I want to be,

For Erin Matherne, who gave a face to *Eating an Elephant,*

For the staff of the Marks Street Senior Recreational Center, who created a home for Writing Your Life . . .

and for my husband Bob Guerrette, who made sure we had good food and clean clothes and kept my life afloat while I wrote; for always making me laugh—I love you.

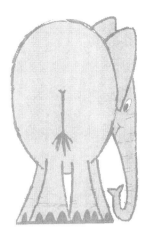

Contents

Eating an Elephant . . .

I tell my students that writing your life story is similar to the 1960s' joke, "How do you eat an elephant?" The answer is by taking one bite at a time, of course. There *is* a way to take this large life you've lived and break it down into manageable pieces. You have decades of material to draw from, yet sometimes having too much information is more difficult than having none at all. The goal of this book is to guide you . . . guide you through putting your story on paper, one step at a time, and provide you with suggestions along the way to improve your writing skills.

You Don't Have To Be a Writer To Write Your Life Story

That's right. You don't have to be a writer to write your life story. This book is written for people who do not believe they have the skill or talent to write. If that's what you think, you're wrong. Ninety-nine percent of the people I work with would not call themselves *writers*, especially the first time they walk into a Writing Your Life classroom, but that hasn't stopped them from writing wonderful, touching, funny stories. They may have some misspelled words or a few grammatical errors, but those things don't make their stories any less endearing.

Anyone can write. Yes, that's what I said; *anyone* can write, even you, shaking your head and saying, "No way possible." Walk with me, and I'll show you how.

So, How Did You Get This Book?

How did this book end up in your hands? Maybe you purchased it to help in writing your life story. In that case, I commend you for the decision to put your life on paper. Bravo!

I do want you to read this book because it will help you, *but*—and this is a big BUT—I want you to write even more. Don't spend all your time reading these pages to avoid writing all those wonderful stories collecting dust in your memory.

Maybe you received this book as a gift from someone—perhaps an adult child or a grandchild—who desperately wants you to write your story. And it's probably not the first do-it-yourself, memoir-writing book you've been given. Furthermore, this one may be destined to take its place on the bookshelf next to the others, or you may hide it away at the top of the closet, not wanting to feel a pang of guilt every time you see it. But it doesn't have to be that way. You *can* write your life story, and I *can* help.

I work with people who come to our initial meeting, carrying folders filled with *attempts* at writing their life stories. Most of the time, their paragraphs bear dates that go back ten years or more. I ask them, "What happened? Why did you stop writing?" The response is usually that they lost interest, didn't know what to do next, ran out of time, the dog ate their draft, whatever. One man told me his ex-wife burned the first hundred pages of his handwritten memoir after they divorced. Ouch, that hurts.

Writing your life story takes time and energy, but in my experience with helping people capture their memories, *all* have said it was well worth the effort. I've also had the privilege to watch family members receive a loved one's book as a Christmas, Hanukah, birthday or anniversary gift. Pure delight and excitement spread across the faces of the recipients, usually followed by a few happy tears and lots of hugs.

In 2005, I decided to write the story of how my parents met and married and give it to them as an anniversary present, but I wanted it to be a surprise, for both of them. I called my dad in South Louisiana and told him I wanted to write their story as a gift for Mom, but I wanted it to be a surprise, so I asked if we could keep our conversations secret. One on board. The next day I called my mom and gave her the same pitch. She wholeheartedly agreed, and off we went into the land of taped telephone conversations, transcriptions and fashioning a story from these interviews. Their stories agreed on all the main points, but you would never have known they shared the same experiences based on the details they gave me. This made the book really humorous.

The day before their anniversary party, I sat with my mom and dad and handed them a beautifully wrapped present. They both looked at each other in such a smug way and tried to convince the other one to open the package. Finally, Mom did the honors, and they soon realized they *both* had been duped. My mother began to cry. I cried. Dad laughed and said, "I'll be *damn*," and a copy of their book was passed around to family and friends. Years later, the book still makes the rounds at family gatherings. Someone pulls it down from the bookshelf, and the story is told one more time.

Don't you think a little effort on your part is well worth bringing the people you love this level of joy? I do.

What Is a Story?

Just so we all understand one another, I need to define one term—*story*. Our friend, Mr. Webster, describes *story* as "a narrative, either true or fictitious, in prose or verse, designed to interest, amuse, or instruct the hearer or reader; tale." Story, the way I use it throughout this book, represents an anecdote that is true to the author's memory. Some writing purists state that a piece of writing called a *story* makes it a work of fiction. Not so.

You'll notice I said *true to the author's memory*. That doesn't mean everyone involved will agree on the details. They probably won't. If five people witness a car accident today, there will be five different versions of what happened tomorrow. Now add thirty, forty, fifty or more years to color people's memories, and no one agrees. I love what my buddy, Loyd, tells his critics, "Go write your own book. This is my memory and my story."

Let's Talk Cajun

I grew up in South Louisiana, and many of the examples I use in this book are sprinkled with Cajun words and sayings. Just in case you're not familiar with these words, here are a few definitions:

andouille—type of flavorful pork sausage

Atchafalaya Basin—located in South Central Louisiana, the Atchafalaya Basin comprises the wetlands surrounding the Atchafalaya River and is the largest swamp in the United States

bateau—French word for a *boat*

bayou—stream or small river with a slow-moving current

boudin—unique Cajun sausage made of pork, rice, onions and seasonings and put into a casing

ça c'est bon! or *c'est bon!*—literally *that's good*

Cajun—descendent of the original Acadian people, exiled from Acadie (now Nova Scotia) in the mid-1700s, who settled in South Louisiana *c'est tout!*—literally *that's all*

Charenton—small community nestled deep in South Louisiana bayou country located one hundred miles southwest of New Orleans, also my hometown

chère—term of endearment like *dear*

courtbouillon—a fish stew made with a red gravy and served over white rice

crawfish—freshwater crustacean that resembles a small lobster—also spelled *crayfish*

étouffée—literally *choked* or *smothered*—a popular Cajun dish made with shellfish, especially crawfish, or chicken in which the meat and seasonings are cooked down slowly into a stew that is served over rice

fais do-do—literally *to make sleep*—country dance where adults brought their children along and put them to sleep nearby while they danced away the night—in modern times, a *fais do-do* is a street dance

filé—powdered sassafras leaves used to season and thicken Cajun *gumbo*

goujon—yellow catfish found in freshwater

gumbo—Cajun delicacy—a spicy stew or soup that usually includes shellfish, sausage, chicken and/or okra, seasoned with the *Cajun trinity:* celery, bell pepper and onion

jambalaya—Cajun dish made of rice, meat or shellfish and seasonings

Jolie Blonde—literally *pretty blond*—popular French song about a fair-haired girl who runs off with another man, often called the Cajun national anthem

king cake—a doughnut-type cake popular during Mardi Gras that has a small, plastic baby baked inside—the person who finds the baby in his/her piece of cake is then required to buy the next cake

lagniappe—a little something extra, an unexpected bonus

mais non—literally *but not,* common Cajun saying

Mardi Gras—Fat Tuesday—Shrove Tuesday, celebration on the day before the start of Lent on Ash Wednesday—the day is usually filled with parades, masked costume balls, rich food and much merriment

Mon Dieu—literally *My God*, common French saying

nonc—abbreviated French word for *uncle*

pogy—fish also called *menhaden* used to bait crawfish traps

tante—French word for *aunt*

très bien—literally *very good*

So, are you ready? Then let's go, step-by-step, one bite of that elephant at a time.

Get Started

Bite #1
The Only Way To Do This Wrong Is To NOT Do It at All!

I write my motto at the top of the board at every class I teach and every talk I give: *The only way to do this wrong is to not do it at all!* I do it to let people know that whatever they put to paper in whatever form they choose will work. Most people don't even try to write their life stories for fear of doing it wrong. We all have a ninth-grade English teacher sitting on our shoulders, red pen in hand, whispering in our ears, "What makes you think you can write? See, there's a dangling participle here. You have comma splices throughout your paper." (What is a comma splice anyway?) The only way to silence that critical voice is to write your way through it.

Just looking at the 1,000-plus pages of the Bible of writing rules and regulations, *The Chicago Manual of Style: The Essential Guide for Writers, Editors, and Publishers,* is reason enough to put your pen and paper away and go take a nap. When driving, we need yield signs, green lights and turn signals to keep us in the road. Likewise, good grammar and punctuation are important in that they help us understand one another, but we don't need to get so hung up on the details that we come to a standstill in bumper-to-bumper traffic. Keep your eyes on the road—your life story—and move forward at a steady speed.

Bite #2
It's Personal

There are as many ways to write life stories as there are people to write them. One man in my class did nothing but make lists. Each day for more than thirty years, he created an accounting of whatever captured his attention for the day—the price of gas, a movie he saw, his wife's birthday present, a new business that opened recently, items in the news, how much he paid for bread. Some days his list had twenty entries, other days only two or three. But he filled his pages consistently in a way that worked for him, and this small action of making a daily list resulted in a treasure trove of historical and personal information.

Over time, I've seen many unique approaches to writing life stories: automobile enthusiasts wrote their memoirs based on the cars they rode in or drove throughout their lifetimes; great cooks dished up family recipes and told the stories behind those delicious meals; artists sketched and wrote scenes they lived; gardeners traced the seasons of their lives with photographs, drawings and descriptions of what grew in their gardens and their lives. Maybe you enjoy a different hobby or interest. How can you use this activity to write your life story?

Bite #3
Don't Try This at Home

I recently heard about a new way to preserve family history from the seventeen-year-old granddaughter of one of my longtime students. After her maternal grandparents died, she and her family moved into her grandparents' home. In this Florida Panhandle residence, they found family history written on the walls of a closet. Someone, probably her grandmother, covered the closet walls with dates of births, deaths, marriages, hurricanes, large purchases and so forth. She and her family continued the tradition and now routinely add new information to these history-filled walls, lending new meaning to the saying: *if only these walls could talk.*

I don't necessarily recommend this method of preserving history—it's very difficult to share or transport walls from one place to another—but it is proof that *how* we write our history is limited only by our imagination. There are as many *correct* ways to write life stories as there are people to write them. What's yours?

Bite #4
Start Anywhere

As I sit here on a cloudy, drizzly, Florida morning, ready to begin writing this book, I feel the need to start at the beginning. Really, it's almost a compulsion. It's what I've been taught throughout all my years of schooling: "Write your thesis sentence first. . . ." But in writing a life story, you set yourself up for failure when you think you have to start at the beginning and write your way through, year-by-year, to the end.

Most of us have brains that do not think in a linear fashion. My mind flits across the decades as easily as I walk from one room into the next. I remember a time I picked figs with Grandpa Luke when I was five years old and that thought takes me to helping Grandma Louisiane make fig preserves when I was ten and on to the time twenty years later, when my parents attempted to ship me fresh figs from their backyard tree (It was a disaster; they arrived as a hot, sour, liquid mass of nastiness.), to the small, plastic container of figs, which cost $9 at the grocery store my husband Bob bought me last week just to see the delight in my face.

Thinking in that jumping-around way is normal, but when it comes to writing, we believe we have to start with, "I was born a very young child . . ." and write our way through to the great barbeque we had with family last Sunday. What are the chances of that happening? The odds are better in Vegas. We get overwhelmed, turn off the computer or put down our pen and go take another nap.

My advice? Start anywhere. Write now, organize later. Write what is on your mind today. If something your spouse says reminds you of a prank you played in high school, write that. If drinking your orange juice at breakfast causes you to remember the sweet smell of orange blossoms on your first trip to Florida when you were six years old, write that. If the baby in a commercial on TV brings back the memory of the birth of your first grandchild, write that. You can't go wrong writing what's on your heart.

Bite #5
Keep an Idea Notebook Handy

Memories pop into our heads at the most inconvenient times—when we're driving, in the shower, in a business meeting, in church. When this happens to me, I tell myself, "Oh that's a great memory. I'll write it down as soon as I get home." What usually happens? You're right. The priceless memory is long gone by the time I pull into the driveway. Sometimes I remember I had a great thought but can't think of what it was. Other times I don't even remember having the thought.

I often tell my friends that I don't have a memory problem; I have a filing problem. I know whatever I need is in my brain, *somewhere;* it's merely misfiled. For example, I'm looking for a memory about my first dog, Shep, under the Ps for pets, and it's filed under the Gs for the Gravy Train I fed him every day. Who knows why? I have to stumble upon it accidentally, but when I do, I don't want to lose it again.

This is my solution to those misfiled memories:

I carry a small notebook and a tiny pen with me everywhere I go, so when I have a memory I don't want to lose, I write down a couple of words that will remind me of it later. Works every time. I suggest you purchase a small notebook (3"x 5") or multiple notebooks, so you can place one in your pocket or handbag, one in the car, one by the bed and wherever else thoughts seem to regularly bubble up to the surface.

Notebooks are great because all the little memory gems are in one place. If I don't use a notebook, I have sticky notes, old receipts, torn off bits of bills, the backs of envelopes, business cards, whatever I can get my hands on, scattered everywhere around my house, in my car, in pants' pockets, in desk drawers, everywhere. And guess what? When I start looking for that memory I wrote down on some piece of scrap paper a week ago, I can't find it. If I write everything in my handy, dandy little notebook, I know right where to go when I need my next writing topic.

Or you can use a technique to keep track of memories my student Judi employs. She often combines writing and eating her lunch. She makes a sandwich, heats up her soup, sits at the kitchen table with her notebook and pen and readies herself to write. On the wall above her kitchen table is a bulletin board covered with memories and story ideas on slips of paper she's accumulated over time. Before she takes the first bite, she chooses a writing topic from the many possibilities tacked to the board, takes in her lunch and pours out her heart.

Bite #6
Hello, Self . . .

If you're driving and you can't pull over or don't want to risk running your car into a light pole while trying to jot down some notes, call yourself on the phone and leave a message. "Hello, Self, I had this great memory. Remind me to write about the time . . ." Then when you get home, you can safely enter the memory in your notebook so the little gift will be there waiting for you when you need it. But if you choose this option, be careful. In some places you can't legally talk and drive at the same time, so pull over and leave that voice message or send yourself a text.

Bite #7
Now Get a Bigger Notebook

Using a large, three-ring binder to organize your stories accomplishes two things at the same time. It helps separate your life into smaller, more manageable segments and painlessly organizes your stories as you write them. Once you have your binder, purchase a package of eight or ten index tabs. Make a tab for each decade of your life, e.g., 1–9 years, 10–19 years, 20–29 years and so forth. After you finish each story, slip it into the section that matches the time period in which the piece takes place. Do this with all your stories, and when you write or type in the last period on the last sentence of the last story, a great deal of your organization will already be completed.

Some of you computer-savvy people reading this may say, "I already do all that in folders on my laptop. Why do I need a notebook?" I'm glad you're organizing your work electronically, but I still suggest you put a hard copy in a binder because you never know what might happen to the computer file. My documents have been corrupted, deleted by mistake and lost; don't ask me how. Having a hard copy saved me more than once.

Plus, with my notebook, I feel a sense of accomplishment that motivates me to keep going as I see the binder, filling with stories. It starts out all skinny and empty, but every story I write plumps it up until it's this big, fat notebook that's a chore to lug around. I hold it in my arms, and I feel the weight of my effort. Go get a binder and watch it grow, sort of like a Chia Pet.

Bite #8
Give It a Name

Your book needs a name, any name. You may have picked one out a long time ago and told yourself, "If I ever write my story, I'm going to call it. . . ." I assisted one gentleman in writing his life story who knew his title was *I Am Blessed*; another said his book must be named *Hoosier Roots*. Great titles. In each case, I printed the title on a sheet of paper in the largest font I had and put the page on the front of the binder. I even printed the title vertically and slid it down the spine of the folder.

A book title may never have crossed your mind. Okay, writing a book may never have entered your mind until now. Either way, it's important to give it a name. It may not be anything like the name you ultimately select, but it needs to be called *something* for a couple of reasons. One, it makes your project easy to identify. You might say, "I'm working on the story of my life from the time I was six years old to when I was twelve years old, growing up in rural Pennsylvania in the 1940s." Whew! That's a mouthful. Or you could simply say, "I'm working on my book titled. . . ."

Bite #9
Make It Real

A more important reason for your life story to be given a name is that it makes it real. It then becomes an entity of its own. Sometimes we say to ourselves, "Who do I think I am writing a memoir?" Well, I have an answer for you. You are a unique individual who has a story that needs to be told, a story that your children, grandchildren and generations to come need to hear. Giving your project a title confirms what you're doing is important.

So, give your book a name and put it on the front of your binder to let the world know this is your life story.

Bite #10
Timeline

We talked earlier about eating an elephant one bite at a time, but first we do have to get a good look at the entire animal. You don't want to get to the end of your story and find out it's missing a tail or that the trunk is in the wrong place. Getting a wide-angle picture of your personal pachyderm, your life, is a good place to begin your project.

One way to do this is by creating a personal timeline imbedded in historically significant U.S. and world events. Don't worry, you do not have to pull out your tenth-grade American history textbook and start taking notes. You can find many excellent U.S. and world history timelines in books or on the Internet. Here are a few that may help:

http://www.infoplease.com/yearbyyear.html

http://www.animatedatlas.com/timeline.html

http://www.ourtimelines.com/create_tl_2c.html

After entering a name and date of birth, this site creates a timeline, telling you the year, the event and the age of the person at the time. See example below. You can also add personal markers like I did here in 1957.

Custom Timeline for Patricia Charpentier		
1965 to 2010		
1946–1989	▬	The Cold War from before birth until age 33
1952–	▬	Reign of Queen Elizabeth II (Windsor) from before birth until after timeline
1953–1960	▪	Dwight D. Eisenhower president of US from before birth until age 4
1956	▮	Ocean liner *Andrea Doria* collides with the Stockholm, sinks at age 0
1957	▮	Patricia has tonsillectomy at age 1
1957	▮	Sputnik launched—1st (artificial) satellite at age 1
1958	▮	Integrated Circuit at age 2
1958	▮	Stereo LP recordings come into usage at age 2
1958	▮	US space agency (NASA) established at age 2
1958	▮	FM Stereo Broadcasts at age 2
1959	▮	Hawaii enters the union—50th at age 3
1959	▮	Alaska enters the union—49th at age 3
1959	▮	1st nuclear powered merchant vessel, *Savannah* at age 3

Bite #11
An Elephant's Eye View

When I say *personal timeline*, I mean whatever period you want to document. I started my timeline with the oldest relatives I remembered as a child, my great-grandparents, Aurestile and Clara (Robicheaux) Hebert, and then came forward to the present day. On the timeline, I marked significant events—births, deaths, marriages, divorces, major moves, job changes, significant illnesses and other life-altering events. My timeline, as expected, became more detailed as I moved into current times. I knew far more about the lives of my parents than I did my great-grandparents and even more about my own life. Creating a timeline is an excellent way to get an elephant's-eye view of your life.

You will likely remember more items as you begin to work on your life story. No problem. Add the new entry to your timeline where it belongs chronologically.

If you have done genealogical research, you can take your timeline back even further. I received a copy of the genealogy of my mother's family back to 1648 when they came from France to settle in Acadie, now Nova Scotia. Once I had that information, I was able to extend my timeline back hundreds of years.

Bite #12
Put It in Context

As you look at your timeline, various themes may surface across the generations like relocations, tragedy, occupations and such. You may see history repeating itself in the choices made. You may see patterns you might not have seen otherwise. You may better understand a time in your life when you see that period in relation to what was going on in the world. For these reasons, and many more, a timeline is a great place to begin.

I wrote Doris' memoir as a gift for my best friend Connie, who is Doris' daughter. When we placed the United States timeline next to Doris' personal history, she understood an important fact. Franklin D. Roosevelt took office the year Doris was born, and he remained president until she approached her teen years. When she realized Roosevelt had been president and a steady presence throughout all her growing up years, Doris understood why his death impacted her life as it did and how it contributed to this unsettled time in her life. This was a conclusion she might not have drawn without putting her life into the context of United States history. Try it; you will see what I mean.

Bite #13
Priming the Pump

When our ancestors said they had to go *prime the pump*, they knew they had to put water into the pump at the well to get the flow started. The same is true for writing our life stories. You have to put in a little effort to get out a lot of memories.

By now, you're probably saying one of two things to yourself: "Wow, I can't believe all the memories flooding my mind. Give me that paper and pen." This is the response we all dream about. If it is yours, put this book down and get going. What are you waiting for?

The more typical response is, "What the heck am I going to write about? I can't even remember what I ate for lunch yesterday." If the second response describes you, don't worry; the memories will come. In my own writing as well as working with others, I find writing your life history is like priming a pump. Once you get the flow started—with water or writing—the rest comes much easier. Start pumping.

Bite #14
Make a List, Part One

Remember your binder? I suggested you separate your life into decades and use dividers to represent each section. Pick one of your decades and make a list—using just a couple of words for each entry—of everything you can remember happening in that time frame. This is a type of brainstorming, and the rules of brainstorming advise you to write as fast as you can for a specified period of time, usually ten minutes or so. Don't stop to think; keep your hand moving. This process works because as you write quickly, you let go of control, and your subconscious is able to slip in a little nugget or two you may not have otherwise remembered.

As an exercise, let's say I picked the years 10-19 of my life to brainstorm. My list might look something like this:

learning to drive	The Franklin Post
living *out of town*	decision to be a journalist
high school	moving away from home
working in the Clerk of Court's Office	going to LSU
falling in love	

Now I have a list of quite a few topics I can write about. I may not end up writing about each entry on my list, but if I need a topic, I can pick from this list. Eventually you'll do this for every decade, but it doesn't all have to be done at one sitting.

Bite #15
Make a List, Part Two

Having this decade list makes writing my life story more manageable. This is how we break down our elephant into bite-sized pieces.

Pick one of the items on your list and repeat the same brainstorming process. Make a list of everything you can remember about that topic. Write quickly. Don't stop to think.

If I selected *high school*, my second list might include:

dance team	bomb threats
football season	riots
Willie Williams	4-H
homecoming court	school plays
marching band	in choir
desegregation	couldn't sing

One more time . . . I select a topic on my second list and jot down everything I can remember about it. Nothing is too small to note. If I choose *marching band* to further brainstorm, my list might look like this:

senior year	bus trips to games
majorette	Mr. Guilbeau
crooked lines	competitions
played no instrument	great drum line

Get the idea? You can continue to pick an item from your list and brainstorm it until you get a list of details specific enough to use in writing your story.

Bite #16
Make a List, Part Three

List-making works on several different levels. A list is much less intimidating than sitting down to a blank page, thinking, *I have to fill up all that white space with something profound.* We make lists every day: to-do lists, grocery lists, packing lists, invitation lists. List-making is not a daunting task.

Final time, I promise . . . select a topic from your last list and brainstorm it, trying to add in as much detail as possible. It's from this list your story will emerge. For example, if I choose the *majorette* topic to write a story about, my detailed list might look like this:

red-sequined uniform	told not to bend down and pick it up during a show
white boots	
team of four	twirled most shows with no baton
Karen, Carrie and Sheila	smiled and twirled air
drove the band leader nuts	did a great job then
couldn't hold onto my baton	

I can take this list and use it in writing sentences and paragraphs to tell a funny story about how bad a majorette I was.

Making a list is one of the best ways I've found to begin eating an elephant. The bites are small, you can eat them quickly and they are easy to digest. Use your list in whatever way works for you. You may write the list, put it aside and never look at it again. That's okay. The very act of putting bites on paper helps organize the details in your mind. Or you may want to use it as a checklist to make sure you didn't leave out some aspect of your story you definitely wanted to include. It's your list. Experiment and figure out how you can best use it. Now, you're ready to write. Go for it!

Bite #17
Writing Rituals

Writing rituals are set behaviors or actions taken at the start of every writing session, and they can be truly helpful. Doing some small task routinely causes the mind to associate it with the act of writing. It alerts the brain that you are ready to put aside the laundry, the television, work and everything else and write. Some look at writing rituals as a way to summon their creativity and tell the muse it's time to get busy.

A writing ritual can be most anything—making a cup of tea, sitting in a certain chair, taking a ten-minute walk, stretching, reading something inspirational, wearing a special item of clothing, meditating, watching birds at the feeder for a few minutes. The action itself is unimportant. The important part is that you do it each time you write.

I remember hearing an author say his writing ritual was sharpening pencils. He used super sharp, No. 2 pencils to write, so before every session, he got out his electric pencil sharpener and put a deadly point on each of his twenty pencils. *Urrrrrrrr, urrrrrrrr, urrrrrrrr, urrrrrrrr.* Something about the sound and the repetition of the task cleared his mind of all worries and responsibilities and prepared him to write. This ritual worked for him.

Bite #18
A Word of Caution

As I wrote a book-length thesis for my master's degree in creative writing, I lit a candle as my writing ritual. I purchased a beautiful, magnolia-scented candle and sat it on my desk. When I was ready to write, I got the matches from the kitchen, listened to the sound as I struck the match on the side of the box, smelled the puff of smoke and the scent of sulphur and watched the spark change into a perfect, orange-yellow flame as I touched it to the candle's wick. The candle remained lit next to my laptop for as long as I wrote. I went through several scented candles before finishing my thesis.

One word of caution . . . be aware if you are going to use fire; it can be danger-ous. The start of writing the thesis coincided with beginning to date my husband Bob in early 2000, so to spend time with me, he brought a book and read while I wrote. On one of those early *thesis dates*, I was too focused on him and pushed my laptop away to chat for a few minutes. The next thing I knew, I smelled plastic burning and saw a small trail of black smoke rising from the back of my laptop screen. I had pushed the screen of my laptop directly over the candle's flame, and it melted a hole into the cover of my computer. Amazingly, the screen worked. I still have that laptop; I keep it as a senti-mental reminder of new love and a warning that my writing can go up in smoke if I'm not careful.

Today I have a much simpler writing ritual. I go to the kitchen, take out my favorite insulated, drinking glass that has a cover with a built-in straw (one of the best pur-chases I ever made), fill it with ice, get a near-frozen, caffeine-free, diet Dr. Pepper out of the refrigerator and slowly pour it into my glass. I love the sound of the ice popping, the fresh smell, the coolness on my face as the carbonated bubbles burst into the air above the cup's rim and that delicious first sip of the chemically-enhanced sweetness of calorie-free, colored water. *Ahhhhhhh* . . . I'm ready to write. Let me at that blank page.

Bite #19
A Writing Schedule

I can already hear you say, "Not another schedule!" I know, I know. Most of our lives are scheduled down to the minute these days. If you're one of the lucky few like my student and friend Elaine who loves to write so much she does it every free minute of every day—in doctors' waiting rooms, at red lights, while she eats, in her sleep—then skip this section. If you're like me, and most other authors I know, writing has to be deliberate; it doesn't happen without a little encouragement from the outside.

No perfect writing schedule exists; you just have to find one which works for you. Maybe you can commit to writing two hours per week. That's great, but make sure you carve out time for yourself because life always tries to encroach on your writing time.

I once had a professor who wrote from 10:00 p.m. when his children went to bed until 1:00 a.m. *every* day. After a few hours of sleep, he got up and worked a full day at his regular job. I couldn't do it, but it worked for him. He wrote and published several award-winning books following this plan.

Instead of a certain number of hours, you may want to commit to writing X number of pages or words each week and not worry about when it gets done. Say you're going to write four, double-spaced pages or 1,000 words each week. You don't commit to a specific time, but even if it means you have to skip your favorite television show (record it) or your Friday night bowling plan, you do it to fulfill the commitment you made to yourself before the week ends. We don't usually have to miss too many events we really want to attend before we fit our writing time in and around other plans.

So, what kind of commitment can you make for the next week? Write it down. Read it every day. And, get busy writing.

Bite #20
Make Yourself Accountable

I have a good bit of discipline for most things, but when it comes to writing, not so much. As much as I love writing, I can be extremely creative at finding reasons to *not* write. The dust bunnies under the bed *need* tending to. I *have* to get the science experiment that was last week's leftovers out from the back of the refrigerator. I *must* answer my e-mails. The world *will* end if I don't make this phone call. Okay, so my excuses aren't so creative, but if I listen to them, I don't write.

One thing that works for me every time is to make myself accountable to someone else. This is where joining a class or writers' group can be a great help. There you are encouraged to write, and you get inspired by the words of others. I always come home ready to write after a class or workshop. Plus, I don't want to be the only one in the group who isn't working on a story. Peer pressure works, and in this case, it works to your advantage.

If I'm not able to join a group of writers, I enlist the help of my friends. I typically make a commitment to friends, Kent and Connie, that I'm going to write for a certain length of time or finish a number of pages for the day or week. Then I feel more obligated to do what I committed to, because they *will* sit on me if I try to weasel out of it. That's the key. Choose support people who care enough to remind you of your commitment if you don't live up to your promise.

I remember reading about how nineteenth-century, French author Victor Hugo made himself accountable to write for a certain amount of time each day. At the appointed hour, he went into his study, took off all his clothes and handed them to his butler with instructions to not return them until the end of his writing time. Granted, this method is a bit drastic, but it obviously worked. Hugo wrote many, many classics, including *Les Miserables* and *The Hunchback of Notre Dame* by making himself accountable, albeit in the nude. Hopefully, you won't have to go to such lengths to get your writing done, but if you do, Victor Hugo's method is always an option.

Bite #21
Plowing Up the Past

My students, Jane and Loyd, are blessed with vivid and detailed memories back to when they were three years old. What a gift! Others, like me, are not so lucky. Some days remembering what I went to the grocery store to purchase is a big challenge. But many tricks designed to reclaim all those wonderful stories from times past exist for people with less than perfect memories.

If possible, take a trip to the area you are writing about and visit the people and places that populated your life. Talk to relatives and friends. Walk through the halls of your old high school. Take a dip in your favorite swimming hole. Eat at the local diner. Immerse yourself in your past, and the memories will join you.

Bite #22
Alternative Trips

What if you can't go back home or the places of your childhood no longer exist? Then take a photographic trip. Pull out the old albums and slowly examine each photograph. Ask yourself questions about what you see. Who are the people? Where was this taken?

When was it taken? What was the occasion? What else do you remember about this time or place?

In addition to looking at the main subject in the photograph, look at the background because the seemingly insignificant items may tell you a great deal about the time and place. What were people wearing? What types of cars did they drive? Is it a rural or city background? Are signs, billboards or advertisements visible? Then look for what's *not* in the picture. Who should be there and isn't? Who was taking the picture? What buildings aren't in the photo? Which ones are there now?

Bite #23
Time Traveler

What if no photographs of your childhood exist? It would be a big loss, but it doesn't mean you can't go back to where you grew up. Instead, you can take a mental trip to the time and place you wish to write about. Find a quiet area, sit with your feet on the floor and your eyes closed. Take a couple of deep breaths and put yourself back into the desired event.

In your mind's eye, slowly look around. Who is present? What does the place look like? What is going on there? What can you hear? Can you identify a certain scent in the air? Are you eating something tasty? Stay with it; don't jump up too quickly. Open yourself up to whatever memories come to you.

Bite #24
That's Good

Here's another way to transport yourself back in time. Eat the foods you loved, or hated, as a child. My favorite childhood meal was *weenie* spaghetti. My mom cut up hotdogs, mixed them into homemade tomato gravy and poured the heavenly mixture over thick, white spaghetti.

On a recent visit home, I arrived in time for lunch and took a look in the pot on the stove—*weenie spaghetti*. It wasn't as great as I remembered, but the tangy taste of the sauce and the soft pieces of wieners, decorating my noodles took me back to when I was five years old and thought there was no finer food. With that remembrance came other memories I quickly wrote down in my notebook.

Bite #25
Follow Your Nose

Scientific studies prove the sense of smell is connected to memory, more so than all other senses. How many times have you caught a whiff of something and been flooded with memories? Instead of having to wait for a particular scent to find its way to you, you can make it happen.

Say, for example, the only thing you remember about your grandparents' house in the country was the gardenia bush in the backyard. Find gardenia-scented candles, perfumes or oils or go to the flower shop and buy a gardenia (or just smell it for free and leave) and allow your senses to guide you to long-forgotten memories.

If an apple pie baking in the oven reminds you of your mother's kitchen, then bake a pie. Don't have time to do that? Get some type of apple pastry, even a Pop Tart will do, and put it in the toaster oven. Inhale deeply and follow where your nose takes you.

My dad was a carpenter most of my growing-up years. He built houses, but his specialty was custom cabinetry, china closets and other fine pieces of furniture. I loved to be out in the shop with him where he sawed, sanded and planed ordinary wooden boards into works of art. Sawdust covered the concrete floor, and the scent of cut wood permeated the air. Today when I want to write about my dad, I make a quick trip to Home Depot or Lowe's and breathe in the rich, wood smells. I take my notebook with me because forgotten memories are always there waiting.

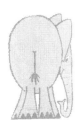

Bite #26
Question Books

Another way to recall memories is to use a book of questions. Many are available today, but my favorite is *To Our Children's Children: Preserving Family Histories for Generations to Come* by Bob Greene and D.G. Fulford. This book contains more than 1,000 questions, which serve as memory joggers.

Books like these are usually divided into chronological categories such as early childhood, teen years, married years, being a grandparent and so forth, or they are more topical in nature, e.g., the house where you grew up, holidays, romance and relationships, food, travels, vehicles, etc.

These books are excellent tools to jog your memory, but they come with a warning. Don't think you have to start with the first question and write your way through to the end. It's too overwhelming and not necessary.

The authors suggest you look at these types of books as you would a menu in a restaurant. When you pick up a menu, you don't think you have to eat everything offered; you pick only what you're in the mood for that day, knowing you'll come back and try something else on another occasion. Use question books in the same manner. Scan the list of entries until one catches your eye, and then begin to write. Write until you feel as though you've exhausted the topic and move on to the next question that looks interesting.

To Our Children's Children is one of the first books of its kind, but quite a few of these helpful volumes are now available, including *Legacy: A Step-by-Step Guide to Writing Personal History* by Linda Spence and *The Book of Myself: A Do-It-Yourself Autobiography in 201 Questions* by Carl and Dale Marshall—get ready for the shameless plug—or you can purchase *my* book of prompts titled *Focus on Writing: I Remember,* taken from a writing workshop I teach every month. You can also find many subject lists on the Internet. Most all of these sources provide the same basic information, so pick one and start writing.

Bite #27
What No One Wants To Talk About

This is a topic no one wants to talk about, but it's important. I won't end this section on a down note, but I do need to remind you that we don't have an unlimited supply of time to write our life stories. Whether we want to think about it or not, we all have a finite number of days on this earth. Most of us do not know when we are nearing that final breath, so we can't delay writing our life stories.

I know of many unfortunate situations where people delayed writing life stories and left their families with a few bits and pieces or nothing at all. One person I know was training for one of his many marathons and had a massive stroke, leaving him unable to speak or write. A longtime class member, Sharon, died suddenly while recuperating from a successful hip replacement and rehabilitation. Not long ago, we said goodbye to another of our dear class friends, Joan. Joan was in good health, sitting at her PC, working on her genealogy in the living room when her husband heard a noise, walked into the room and found her slumped over the keyboard, having suffered a massive stroke.

Rollin heard me speak at a genealogy conference and picked up my business card in case he needed my services one day. Three years later, he called and told me he had been diagnosed with terminal cancer, and he no longer had the time to finish his genealogy research and write his personal and family history. He hired me to do the writing.

For the next year, in the midst of his chemotherapy and radiation treatments, we worked on his story. Toward the end, I believed it was this writing project that was keeping him alive. He died a few months after we finished his book, but he lived to give copies to his children and grandchildren and the genealogical and historical societies that helped him compile his family history.

I won't belabor the point, but I hope you get the message. We all know we're going to die, but we always think it won't be today or tomorrow. Get busy writing your life story, and then you won't have to worry.

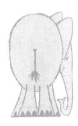

Bite #28
A Better Reason To Get Started

Here's an even better reason to not delay. Sharing your life story with family members has so many benefits, I can't even begin to list them all here. Again and again, people who have written their stories tell me they've had conversations with their children on topics that otherwise would never have been discussed. Adult children tell me they learned so much about their parents that they did not know. Grandchildren tell me they never knew Grandpa was anything but a successful businessman.

Years ago, I gave my mother one of those fill-in-the-blank autobiography books, and so far, in all the talks I've given and all the classes I've taught in the last ten years, she is the only one who actually completed it. Go Mom! I learned so much about her, topics I would *never* have thought to bring up. One question asked: "What was the subject(s) I always wanted to learn more about as an adult but never did?" My mom answered that she would have liked to learn to knit, do calligraphy and create stained glass.

For her next birthday, I bought her a left-handed calligraphy kit. (Both my parents are left-handed, and I'm right-handed. You should see the backwards way I tie my shoes.) When she opened the gift, she was amazed, "How did you know?" She had forgotten she wrote this in her book. Over and over again, I used the contents of this book to ask questions, cook her favorite meals, learn more about her aspirations, get to know my mother as a woman, someone other than just *my mom*. I came to appreciate and respect her even more than I did before.

Take the time, make the effort and be repaid tenfold.

Detail & Description

One easy thing to do to improve your writing a hundredfold—yes, I did say easy—is to add a touch of detail and description. Even though there are many approaches to accomplish this, adding detail and description involves just one thing: taking what is general and making it specific. That *flower* becomes a fuchsia zinnia; the *boy* becomes a three-year-old toddler; her *dog* becomes a black standard poodle. Let's look at this business of writing more descriptively a little more closely.

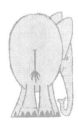

Bite #29
Why Description?

Our goal in adding detail and description to our stories is to create pictures in the mind of the reader. Yes, most anything we write colors the canvas of the reader's mind, but is it in the shade we want, the texture we desire? Does it have the same feel as when we lived it? Chances are it won't; the reader will use her own experience to create the image. That's not a bad thing, but we are telling our stories, and we want the reader to picture our experience, not her own.

Detail and description accomplish other goals as well. They make your story more real, believable and honest. Allowing the reader into your personal experience also creates a sense of intimacy and connectedness that brings decades-old memories to life, transporting the reader back to a time he may not otherwise ever visit.

Adding description is similar to the first time we experienced color television. Some of you younger people have no idea of what I'm talking about, but those of us aged fifty and beyond know exactly what I mean. I was about ten when my parents purchased a color television, and I saw *Bonanza* in Technicolor. I sat three feet from the screen—my mother would not let me sit any closer because she feared the radiation coming off the TV—and scrutinized every detail. I adored Little Joe in any color, but to see his wavy, brown hair and crystal-blue eyes made me fall in love all over again. Detail and description create that kind of memorable reaction.

Bite #30
Not Just Adjectives, Baby

Most people think of adjectives and colorful, flowery language when I encourage them to make a sentence more descriptive. Adjectives, as you may know, are words used to modify nouns. (Learn more about adjectives in Bite #145.) When selected thoughtfully and deliberately, adjectives are great. However, when a writer chooses to load a sentence down with adjectives to make it *descriptive,* that is less than ideal. The poor sentence bears the weight of way too many adjectives; for example:

> Bev's *lovely, happy, elderly* grandmother loved to sing the *old-fashioned, church* hymns she learned as a *small, clever* child in the *beautiful* mountains of Eastern Tennessee.

Whew! That is tough . . . one sentence carrying the load of eight adjectives. What would this sentence look like if we tried to convey the same image with fewer adjectives? Take a look at this:

> Bev's 80-year-old grandmother, whose bright eyes and smooth skin contradicted her chronological age, sang "Amazing Grace" and "The Old Rugged Cross" with as much enthusiasm as she did when she was only five years old, sitting in the pew of her First Baptist Church in Eastern Tennessee.

Okay, the sentence is longer, but now the reader has information that creates a clearer image in his mind. We changed general words to specific ones: *elderly* to *80-year-*

old, lovely to someone who had *bright eyes and smooth skin, old-fashioned, church hymns* to specific song titles, *happy* to *with as much enthusiasm, clever, little girl* to *only five years old.*

Take the general and make it specific. Whenever possible, replace adjectives with concrete nouns.

Bite #31
Trade Adverbs for Better Verbs

Next to adjectives, writers tend to use adverbs to make their stories more descriptive. Again, adverbs are not bad; there are just better ways to add pizzazz to your sentences. (For more than you probably want to know about adverbs, refer to Bite #144.) Like concrete nouns are better than adjectives, strong verbs accomplish more than adverbs.

Adverbs are those words we sometimes use to spice up a *blah* verb. Most of the time, you can spot an adverb by its "ly" ending. Here are a few examples:

She walked *slowly* up the hill.
He *thickly* spread butter on his biscuit.
She *truly* loved him.

Okay, that's not all bad. I've seen worst crimes committed in the name of writing. But compare those examples to these:

She *trudged* up the hill.
He *slathered* butter on his biscuit.
She *adored* him.

So, what do you think? Better? You *betcha.* Isn't *slathered* the best word? I have an immediate visual of the fluffy, white insides of a biscuit and a kitchen knife loaded with creamy butter gliding across the surface of those two halves of heaven. It's enough of a visual to make me hungry. That's the effect we're after. Make the reader want to get up and pull out the box of Bisquick or at the very least, drive down to Popeye's Fried Chicken.

Let me reiterate, so I don't get the reputation of being an adjective and adverb hater;

they are great parts of speech. I use them all the time, *but* I also make sure there's not a concrete noun or a strong verb I can use instead. (If you do that, I'll *lovingly* accept your *well-chosen* adverbs and adjectives. Hee-hee.)

Bite #32
Sense Appeal

We all have five senses. Quick, name them: sight, sound, taste, touch and smell. Many people say there are six, intuition being the last one. If you agree, by all means, use it in your writing. If we have all these different senses to use, why do we rely so heavily on sight?

I think describing things visually comes more naturally to us. For those of us fortunate enough to have good or corrected eyesight, we rely on the images we see to order our world. It takes more effort to describe people, places and things by our lesser-used senses, but the payoff is well-rounded descriptions in our writing.

Try this. Pick a single image from your childhood and describe it using as many of your senses as possible. You may want to narrow your focus for this exercise. Let's say, I want to describe the one day I spent as a commercial fisherman, helping my dad during Christmas break from college. Here are some of the senses I could incorporate:

Sight—brown water of the Atchafalaya Basin, water hyacinth plants rising two feet higher than the boat, my dad's aluminum *bateau*, red, mesh sacks to place our catch in and so forth. You get the idea.

Sound—the quiet of the early morning, the high-pitched hum of the boat engine, my dad's voice, straining to be heard over the sound of the motor, the frantic flipping of the crawfish tails as we raised the trap from the water, the sound of raindrops hitting the water

Smell—oh, I'll never forget this one—rotten *pogy*, bait fish that had to be removed from the trap and replaced with new, smelly pogy, exhaust from the mixture of oil and gasoline used to run the boat motor

Touch—the rough, plastic-coated wire of the traps, the wet line used to pull up the traps from the bottom, the cold of the aluminum boat, the frosty air of the December morning, the cold rain that fell most of the day

Taste—the salty, meaty taste of bologna and tangy mustard sandwiches we brought for lunch, the taste in my mouth of that nasty bait fish I breathed in all day long and couldn't get rid of for days

I might not use all those details in the story I'd write, but even if I used half of them, wouldn't the description of that day be incredibly rich in detail? You bet. I could put you right in the middle of the boat with my dad and me and have you smelling the rotten fish before long. That is the power of including all the senses in your writing and not relying only on sight.

And in this case, I used my sense of intuition when I decided commercial fishing in the wintertime was not for me. It took me only one day to be ready to hit the books again.

Bite #33
Put It in Context

Another way to add detail to your story is to put it into the context of time and place, and to do that, you don't necessarily have to say, "This happened in 1955" or "My cousin lived in Texas." Using iconic images and well-known moments in history ground your story and give the reader subtle yet clear clues about place and time.

If I refer to Elvis' hit single, "Blue Suede Shoes" playing on the turntable, you would probably place the story in the 1950s, and you'd be correct. When writing about a vacation taken with my family as a child, if I mention the Alamo not being as large as I expected, you'd know I was in Texas. See what I mean? This is merely another way to layer detail and bring your story to life.

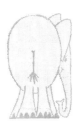

Bite #34
Smile, It's a Simile

Simile looks like the word *smile*—and good similes always make me smile—but a simile is a figure of speech that compares two distinctly different things using the words *like* or *as* and is an effective form of description. Let me show you. We read the memoir, *Ava's Man* by Rick Bragg, in a recent class and so enjoyed Bragg's extensive use of fresh similes. Here are a few examples from his book:

> still *as* a cement angel
> [Fury] rode his shoulder *like* a parrot.
> His temper was hot *as* bird's blood.
> arms like iron and fingers *like* rivets
> as popular *as* an itch
> He went out soft and quiet, *like* a cat leaving a room.

Aren't those great? What makes them great is the vividness of the language. His similes bring immediate images to our minds, and they are fresh pictures, not the tired, worn out clichés: *She was as pretty as a picture, as sweet as candy.* There is a reason clichés come to us so easily; we've heard them a thousand times. Sometimes we have to dig down three or four levels to get past the ever-ready clichés and find an original description. Your reader will love your efforts.

Bite #35
Meta What?

A metaphor is similar to a simile in that it compares two unlike items, but instead of drawing a comparison by using *like* or *as,* it states that the subject *is* something else. Here are a couple of metaphors from Rick Bragg's book, *Ava's Man:*

when life *is* electric blankets and peach ice cream.

Home *was* the driveway, any driveway, that they saw their daddy walk up in the cool of the evening.

books *were* a secret, locked up tight.

Here Bragg is saying life is the same thing as blankets and peach ice cream, home is a driveway and books are a secret. Sometimes an author has a difficult time communicating a complex idea to the reader. Using a metaphor takes what may not be easily understandable and compares it to something more ordinary like blankets, ice cream, driveways and secrets.

Bite #36
Describe This

Try this. Make a list of similes you could use to describe an undisciplined little boy. Write down those clichés that have already popped into your head just to get them out of the way. Now, think about what original images you could use to describe how bad this kid is. Don't hold back. Write each one on your pad of paper. You will likely throw most of them away, but one may ring true and bright.

The little boy was as bad *as*...

The bad little boy was *like*...

Characterization

You have characters in your life story, and I don't mean Uncle Arthur who wears his clothes inside out and quotes Shakespeare at the bowling alley on Saturday night. Most families have at least one of those. When writing your life story, *all* the people who populate your life are characters. And guess what? You're the main character. If your readers are fortunate enough to know the people you're writing about, that's great. They already understand what they look like, how they talk and their peculiar mannerisms, but what about the generations to come that will never meet these people? It is your job as a writer to breathe life into those who live on your pages. How do you do this? It's not as difficult as you might think. Follow along with me.

Bite #37
Who Are They?

The first thing I suggest is making a list of the major players in your life. These change over time, so do it by decade. Take the age group, 0–9 years. Your list might look something like this:

Mom	Uncle Jerry
Dad	Aunt Flo
Grandma	Jolene, my best friend
Grandpa	Miss Veeder, first grade teacher

Mr. Mixon, principal
Uncle Benny, close family friend
Curt, my first boyfriend

Randy, a neighborhood friend
David, Randy's annoying little brother

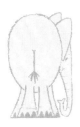

Bite #38
Profiling

You may be asking yourself, how do I reduce a living, breathing human being into a few words? It may take more than a few words to bring that person to life on the page, but usually, you don't have to go on and on to provide the reader with a sense of who someone is.

Guess how I advise you to start? You got it; make a list. If you haven't already noticed, I'm a big fan of lists. Through this task, you will begin to create a character profile. Pick a character you wish to describe. You may want to start with a person who played a smaller role in your life and save the biggies like Mom and Dad for when you get more comfortable doing this.

In describing Miss Veeder, my list looks like this:

Approximately 5' 8"
Medium build
Soft, gray eyes
Mixture of brown and gray hair
Short hair, curly at the ends
Eyes closed to slits when she smiled
Wore long skirts and white blouses
Usually wore a decorative pin
Gap between her two front teeth
Stood very straight
Liver spots on her hands

Gave lots of encouragement
Spoke in a low voice, never shouted or
    yelled
Hugged us all everyday
Shied away from the limelight
Teacher for 37 years
Graduated from college in 1931
Taught for 31 years in same classroom
Taught both my mother and me
Never married

Notice that the list contains a variety of different types of description. There is some physical description (hair and eye color, gap in front teeth, height, build), some information about her disposition (low voice, modest, affectionate) and some background details (graduated from college in 1931, 37 years in teaching, taught multiple generations). Let's look at each one of those aspects a little more closely.

Bite #39
What Do They Look Like?

Usually describing the looks of someone you know well is the easiest way to begin. Start your list with the obvious: height, weight, build, hair and eye color. Then detail other, more subtle aspects of her appearance. For example, describe the shape of her face, what she wore, jewelry, her posture, the color of her skin, any scars or defects, birthmarks and so forth. Write down what you observe when looking at this person, either in real life or in your mind's eye.

I want to encourage you to be as specific as possible when characterizing someone. Say for example, you want to describe someone's smile. Sounds easy enough, right? But is it? Think about all the different kinds of smiles you've seen—a toothless smile, a closed-mouth, a Mona Lisa smile, a smile that shows lots of gum, a gap-toothed smile, a smile with dimples, a smirk. Get the idea? Be specific in describing a person's features.

Bite #40
What Do They Sound Like?

Think about the tone of this person's voice. Is it high pitched or deep like a baritone singer? Does she talk extremely fast like the guy in the old FedEx commercial, or do her words come . . . out . . . one . . . at . . . a . . . time? Does she consistently mispronounce certain words? Does she have an accent? Does she repeat certain sayings?

My friend Jennifer has a special way she ends every telephone conversation. She always says, "Take good care." I hear "take care" all the time, but she's the only person I know who says "take *good* care." I love knowing that little detail about her, and I wait to hear her signature phrase before we hang up. If I were to write about Jennifer, I'd work that expression into the story because it characterizes her.

Look for anything unique about the person's speech. How he sounds and what he says reveal a great deal about the person's level of education, attitude and disposition. Make use of it.

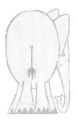

Bite #41
What Do They Do?

What a person does also characterizes him. His profession is one part of what he does, but there's so much more. Visualize the person you wish to write about, then make a list of what you see. You may remember certain gestures, tics, physical habits like biting his fingernails or drumming on every flat surface or always sitting cross-legged in a chair. What were his hobbies? What did he like to do on his day off? Did he have certain facial expressions? What did he have with him always—a small dog, a big cigar, a walking cane, a pocketful of change, which he jiggled constantly? I always notice when someone does this because it drives me nuts!

To get into the habit of *seeing* people in this way, you may want to do some discrete people-watching at the local mall. Observe the patterns of behavior. See what they do repeatedly. Study the looks on their faces as they pass by.

Like a person's speech, his mannerisms, body language, hobbies, routines and profession may expose a great deal about him.

Bite #42
Tell Me Something Interesting

My husband Bob and I joined a group of twenty friends for a backyard cookout. Sitting around a long table, someone suggested everyone tell some interesting fact or story about him or herself.

Many of us knew one another for ten, fifteen years or more, but we were amazed at the new things we learned. Joyce used to be a speed roller skater. Brian learned how to speak some Russian while at the Air Force Academy, and it came in handy when a Russian commander flew with him on a combat mission. Jenn's dreams of fame were slashed when she didn't get cast in her eighth-grade, school musical, *Bye Bye Birdie*. I told about an incredible encounter with a 350-pound grouper while scuba diving beneath an oil rig platform one hundred miles out in the Gulf of Mexico.

When writing about a person, look for what is interesting and out of the ordinary. It's always there. Highlight someone's rich, ancestral history. Write about a person's fifteen minutes of fame. Detail a close encounter with some illustrious person. Okay, get started making that list.

Bite #43
How Do They Think and Feel?

Sometimes we can't figure out the workings of our own minds, so how are we supposed to communicate the way someone else thinks or what he believes? Usually you can accomplish this by what he says and what he does. If you write about a person who goes to church every day, your reader will likely deduce he is a religious man who has a faith in God. If your character builds a bomb shelter, stocks it with food and supplies and conducts regular escape drills with his family, the reader will get the idea this person is worried about catastrophic disasters which may bring about the end of the world. Characterize the people in your story by asking yourself some of the following questions:

What does he want?
What does he fear?
What does he believe?
What does he consider important?

Answer these questions with *concrete* examples, and your reader will come to know the person as you do.

Sometimes learning the *why* behind someone's actions helps characterize her and makes for an interesting story. I grew up watching my mom be terrorized by lightning and thunderstorms. When dark clouds loomed, she hid, crouched on the floor in a place in the house where she couldn't see outside, put her hands over her ears and prayed the rosary. My grandmother had the same debilitating fear. When a storm came up in the middle of the night, she got her children up and dressed, and they had to sit on the couch in their raincoats until the bad weather blew over.

No doubt this intense fear in both my mother and grandmother originated with a tornado that ripped through South Louisiana in April 1952 when my mother was in high school. The twister lifted my grandparents' wood-frame home off the blocks with them and their young children inside, spun it around and set it down on the ground approximately thirty feet from where it originally stood. All the windows were blown out, and the inside of the house was in shambles, but thankfully no one was seriously hurt.

Oddly in the midst of the chaos, the cup of coffee my grandfather had just poured sat on the table as he left it, missing not one drop. The basket of fresh eggs my grandmother had on top of the deep freezer also survived without one crack.

If I want to describe my mother's fear and the actions she took during a thunderstorm, the information just discussed should be communicated in some way to fully tell the story and characterize my mother.

Bite #44
Disposition

When we say people are *uptight* or *laid back* or *easygoing* or *way too stiff*, we're talking about their general disposition. This is usually an important characteristic to convey because it helps the reader understand the actions taken or not taken by the person in response to a variety of situations.

Disposition is a *habitual* inclination or tendency, so there should be plenty of incidents available to describe this aspect of a character's personality. I encourage you to include some examples of disposition in your story instead of merely saying my brother is laid back or my sister is uptight. *Laid back* and *uptight* mean different things to different people. Showing examples of this trait in action explains the character much better than merely stating it as fact. To portray *nervous* or *jumpy,* these actions could be used:

sat for only five minutes before jumping up

flipped through the TV channels

read a magazine while working on a laptop and watching TV

walked fast

talked fast, didn't complete thoughts

changed topics mid-sentence

Does that help explain how to show a person's demeanor rather than simply stating it?

Bite #45
That's So Unique

I've given you many different ways to characterize a person, but you don't have to use each approach on every person. If you do, it's likely you'll never finish your book. Here's the trick: when characterizing someone, look for what is *unique*. If a person's hair is brown, like millions of other people in the world, then you may want to omit that detail and look more closely to find something original. Was her hair brown except for the iceberg-white streak running through it since she was five years old? Or was her hair coarse and bristly like the hair on an elephant? Think about what stands out, what makes the person unique and write that.

Bite #46
A Picture Is Worth a Thousand Words, But . . .

Like the old saying goes, "A picture is worth a thousand words," but as writers, we cannot rely solely on photographs. You may include photographs in your life story, and I strongly encourage you to do so, but don't depend on the image to do all the work.

Describe each photograph in detail in the body of the text. What you see may be totally different from what someone else sees. Also, many of the old photographs we include are black and white, so a woman's dark hair may be brown, red or black. We can't tell from the picture, so you need to tell the reader what he or she needs to know.

Bite #47
A Portrait in Words

Your turn. If you haven't done so already, fire up your computer or pick up your pen and make a list of attributes that describe someone in your life story. Get the physical characteristics out of the way first and then look at this person more closely. Pay attention to other traits—speech, disposition, behaviors, routines, scents, beliefs and so forth.

Dialogue

At its most basic, dialogue is a conversation between two or more people. Most people think dialogue represents the *exact* words spoken by the individuals. When I worked for newspapers, it was critical that I get the person's exact words, so I could quote him accurately. Dialogue is somewhat different. Dialogue, as it is used in writing life stories, is a *reconstruction* of a conversation. This exchange might have been five minutes or fifty years ago. Either way, it's still going to be reconstructed.

The gift of recounting exactly what was said verbatim is unique. Most of us cannot do this, but even if we could, I don't think we should. I'll tell you why later. If we don't have a transcript of the conversation, we reconstruct it to the best of our ability based on what we know about the person and the situation.

No, this is not cheating, lying or pulling one over on the reader. We don't make up conversations that never took place. If I wrote dialogue, which recalled a discussion between President Harry S. Truman and myself at the White House, that would be an outright fabrication. I wasn't born until three years after Truman left office. But when I write a conversation my mother and I had when I was thirteen, I probably won't remember our exact words, but I do know basically what was said, and I know my mother well enough to choose words she most likely used.

Coming to terms with the legitimacy of writing dialogue is something every writer must work out for him or herself. I strongly urge you to do this, because, as we'll see in future elephant bites, dialogue can bring a story to life more so than any other tool in the writer's bag.

Bite #48
Why Dialogue?

One of my students, Becky, loves to write dialogue. It flows from her pen naturally, and she finds it difficult to *not* write her stories in dialogue. She's the exception.

Many writers cringe at the thought of dialogue. They only want to tell the story; they don't want to create all these conversations. And you can do that. Not having dialogue doesn't make it bad writing, but I strongly believe including it in your story makes the writing much better. "Why?" you ask.

Dialogue accomplishes many things. One of the most important reasons to use dialogue is that it helps define the character speaking. Reading someone's words can reveal many details about the person—his education level, where he is from, her occupation, her status in life, his view of the world, just to name a few. This is achieved by choosing precise words. For example, a character might say:

> "I *pert near* got chomped on by an alligator last time I went froggin'," Cousin Bobby
> Joe said.

What does this quote tell about the character? For starters, he's probably from the South, lives near water and is an outdoorsman. How do you know? By how he speaks and the words he uses, of course.

Another reason to include dialogue is because hearing the character's words creates a sense of intimacy and credibility. The words are coming directly from *the horse's mouth*, to use an old cliché, establishing a connection between the character and the reader. Unless the character has proven to be untrustworthy, we typically give an extra measure of believability to what the person is saying as opposed to what the author is summarizing.

Bite #49
Breaks Up the Gray Matter

Of all the good reasons to include dialogue in your story, this one would not likely be at the top of the list, but it is still important. Adding dialogue breaks up the gray on the page and makes it easier on the eyes of your reader. If you have no dialogue, no line breaks and long paragraphs, you will end up with a gray mass on each page. My mom told me she won't even read a book if it doesn't have dialogue, so if you want my mother and others like her to read your stories, you best include some conversation.

Bite #50
Get Real

Since dialogue is reconstructed speech, you want to make sure what your character says is congruent with who he is. You don't want to put words in his mouth that he *never* would say. For example, I would not expect a ninety-year-old grandmother to talk about a favorite rap song she downloaded to her iPod temporarily until she receives the iPad her son ordered for her. I'm sure there is someone out there for whom these actions would fit perfectly, *but* she would be the exception. Make sure the words you choose are specific to the individual's age, educational level, background and so forth.

Read the following line of dialogue and see if you can determine what kind of person said it:

> "Miss Spencer, I take my tea precisely at 3:00 p.m. with two *biscuits* served on my late *mum's* silver tray and placed on the corner of the Tudor desk in my library after which I will take a *kip*, so please do not disturb me. Now run along. *Ta.*"

What do you think? To me, this person sounds like an older man, British, committed to a specific routine, educated, a tad controlling, upper class, wealthy. The portrait this dialogue creates depends on select words (*biscuits, mum, kip, ta*) to establish nationality, specific details (precise time and location) to show his daily routine, a desk and library indicate education, having a servant and using a silver tray alludes to wealth. Always remember: a few well-chosen words convey a stronger message than pages and pages of vague words.

Bite #51
Pick Up the Pace

We'll talk later about pacing—keeping your story moving and not letting it bog down— but for now, know that using dialogue picks up the speed of the tale you are telling and that is usually a good thing. Dialogue tends to be a series of short sentences, containing fewer words than traditional sentences, and a back and forth between two or more people, so those pages are much faster reads. Most of the time, the character doesn't go on and on and on without the interruption of another speaker or something happening. A character here and there in our story may do just that, but then it's called a *monologue*, not dialogue.

For example, read the following at a normal pace:

"*Mais, chere,* guess what I heard today?" Pierre asked.

"What's that?" said Marie.

"T'Joe is king of Mardi Gras this year."

"*Mon Dieu,*" Marie said. "I thought he was dead."

"No, *chere,* not yet."

"How's he gonna get up on the float?" Marie asked.

"Don't know. Maybe a winch."

With shorter sentences of fewer words and a back and forth between two or more people, the speed of our reading quickens. You'll notice when you go back to reading straight prose, you settle into a slower rhythm. Inserting dialogue within your story helps keep the reader on his toes because the pace speeds up and slows down, and he has to be ready for the changes.

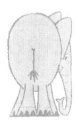

Bite #52
He Said/She Said

I'm going against a generally accepted writing rule—not repeating the same word in the same or adjoining sentences. *Said* is a great word and can be used over and over without the reader tiring of it. It doesn't stand out; we read right through it. Using a scattering of words like *asked, questioned, remarked, stated* also works, but if you try to be clever and see how many different tagline words you can come up with, it will draw the reader's attention away from what is being said. Read this:

> "*Mais, chere,* guess what I heard today?" Pierre questioned.
> "What's that?" exclaimed Marie.
> "T'Joe is king of Mardi Gras this year," disclosed Pierre.
> "*Mon dieu,*" Marie declared. "I thought he was dead."
> "No, *chere,* not yet," Pierre affirmed.
> "How's he gonna get up on the float?" Marie wondered.
> "Don't know. Maybe a winch," Pierre supplied.

What has your attention in this bit of dialogue? Chances are you're focused on the words used in the taglines—*questioned, exclaimed, disclosed, declared, affirmed, wondered, supplied*. Nothing is wrong with those words; they are great words, but overdone, it sounds amateurish. Using *said* with every line, although unnecessary in this example, does not intrude upon the content of the conversation:

> "*Mais, chere,* guess what I heard today?" Pierre said.
> "What's that?" said Marie.
> "T'Joe is king of Mardi Gras this year," Pierre said.
> "*Mon dieu,*" Marie said. "I thought he was dead."
> "No, *chere,* not yet," Pierre said.
> "How's he gonna get up on the float?" Marie said.
> "Don't know. Maybe a winch," Pierre said.

You are probably wondering who is T'Joe, why was he selected as king of Mardi Gras, how old the guy is, why can't he get up on the float, which means your focus is on what is being said, not the taglines. Bingo!

Bite #53
New Speaker, New Paragraph

This bite is an easy one, but both new and experienced writers forget it sometimes. Every time you change speakers, start a new paragraph. I know . . . it wastes a lot of space, but good reasons exist for following this standard. First, it alerts the reader that a different character is speaking, and second, if the dialogue is composed of short sentences, it breaks up the gray matter on the page with white space. Just remember—new speaker, new paragraph, always, forever, every time.

Bite #54
Hey You . . .

Direct address, using someone's name in the dialogue, is a useful tool and can help the reader keep track of who is speaking in long sections of conversation. But, like most of the topics we've talked about so far, it can get tiresome and darn right aggravating if used too much. How would you feel hearing this discussion?

> *"Mais,* Marie, guess what I heard today," Pierre said.
> "What's that, Pierre?" said Marie.
> "T'Joe is king of Mardi Gras this year, Marie," Pierre said.
> *"Mon Dieu,* Pierre," Marie said. "I thought he was dead."
> "No, Marie, not yet," Pierre said.
> "Pierre, how's he gonna get up on the float?" Marie said.
> "Don't know, Marie. Maybe a winch," Pierre said.

It sounds contrived, doesn't it? We don't talk this way, so we shouldn't write our dialogue that way either. Do a little constructive eavesdropping next time you're at a restaurant or coffee shop, some place where you can listen to a conversation you are not a part of. Jot down what's said if possible or listen closely. You may hear a few direct addresses, but it won't be anything like the example above.

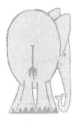

Bite #55
Not Just Talking

When we have a conversation with someone, we rarely *just* exchange words. We don't stand there with our arms at our sides, stiff as cypress planks, only moving our lips. We scratch our noses, tug on our pants, chew gum, shift our weight from one leg to the other, furrow our brows and so forth. So, why don't we add those little nuances into our written conversation? We should because it makes what's being said more authentic. It gives us a clearer picture of what is going on in the conversation.

> "There's a *fais do-do* at the park tonight," Kelly said. "Would you like to go with me?"
> He looked down and rolled a rock around with his shoe.
> "Why, I'd love to go, *chère,*" Eunice said, tilting her head to catch his eye. "You're the best dancer in town."
> Kelly raised his head as a huge smile overtook his face. "Hot dang! I'll pick you up at seven."

Based on this conversation between Kelly and Eunice, what does the body language tell you in addition to their words? One, Kelly is probably shy, unsure of himself and doesn't expect Eunice to say "yes" to his request, and two, Eunice appears to like Kelly and acts in a kindly manner toward him.

Adding small gestures and actions to your dialogue is the best way possible to make it authentic and believable. Like Mikey, "Try it; you'll like it."

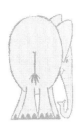

Bite #56
Say What You Mean

Another benefit of *showing* the speaker's actions is giving the reader an opportunity to determine the sincerity of what is being said. A speaker's gestures may well contradict the words spoken. If we don't *see* those signals, we miss the intent of the conversation. For example,

> Cotton said, "My seafood *gumbo* is the best at the cookoff."
> "You're certainly right about that," Mercedes said, turning her head away and rolling her eyes.

Without being informed of Mercedes' actions after what she said, the conversation has a totally different meaning. Allow your reader to see as well as hear.

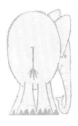

Bite #57
Doesn't Have To Be Lengthy

When you compose dialogue, you don't have to always write a long, ongoing conversation. A few lines may be plenty enough to make your point. Even three or four, well-chosen, back-and-forth sentences serve to break up the text, characterize the speakers and quicken the pace.

Bite #58
Your Turn

Try your hand at whipping up some dialogue. Think of a conversation you had with someone recently. Write down the meat of what was said, only a few lines. Dispense with all the niceties and the *you knows*. Let us know who is talking, and remember to start a new paragraph with each speaker.

Bite #59
Let the Reader Know This Is Important

By choosing to write certain portions of your story in dialogue, you tell the reader, "Hey, this is important. Pay attention." It's not quite like smacking someone with a sack of crawfish, but it's close.

The amount of time an author spends on a topic lets the reader know important information is being shared. We don't go on for pages and pages, writing about the grocery list we made yesterday, at least I hope not. Unless it's one heck of a grocery list, like something you'd make when the President of the United States comes over for dinner, it's a routine task of no great significance.

On the other hand, when we allow the reader to hear the telephone ring, enjoy the happy voice that says *hello,* listen to the first *oh my,* the caller saying *it happened so suddenly, he's sorry, is there anyone he can call,* then I sit up and take notice, knowing the information being communicated in dialogue is critical to the story.

Again, if the writer stops *telling* you what's happening and begins *showing* you, pay attention.

Bite #60
A Way To Not Judge

We're nice people; we don't like to say bad things about others, but sometimes unpleasant situations need to be written about. Instead of *telling* the reader your uncle was a lazy, arrogant, cheap, good-for-nothing sack of bones, you can write dialogue and allow him to show what he's made of. For example:

"Wasn't that a great band, Uncle Ray?" I asked, still humming the final song, *"Jolie Blonde."*

"Humph, great if you like out-of-tune fiddle playing and Frenchmen who sing through their noses. Why don't they just sing in English, for God's sake? This is America," he said.

"It's a Cajun band, *Nonc*; they always sing in French," I said.

"I could get up there and do a better job. Plus it cost me five bucks to get in. What a waste," he replied, shaking his head.

"C'mon Uncle Ray, you are bound to have liked something about it," I said.

"Yeah, I did. I liked when it ended and the thought of getting back to my couch to watch *The Bachelorette.*"

The character of Uncle Ray would have been perceived by the reader differently if I had written:

Nothing ever pleases my Uncle Ray. Even when I try to do something nice for him, like taking him to a Cajun concert, all he does is complain—the band is out of tune, he thinks they sing through their noses, he gripes about the $5 ticket price, he expects a Cajun band not to sing in French, and all he wants to do is go home to his couch and watch *The Bachelorette.* He is such a loser.

See what I mean? The reader may have even sided with the uncle, thinking his niece was talking badly about him, possibly making things up. When it comes from Uncle Ray's mouth, it's a different story. There is no argument.

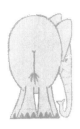

Bite #61
Say It With Meaning

Avoid meaningless exchanges in your dialogue. Bypass all the preliminary niceties; jump right in and get to the heart of the matter. What part of this conversation is more interesting?

"Hi Grandma. What are you doing?" I asked as soon as she picked up the phone.

"Not much. It's good to hear from you, darling," she said. "What have you been up to?"

"Nothing different. Same old stuff," I answered. "How's Grandpa?"

"About the same. No changes since we last talked."

"Is he stable now?" I asked.

"He seems to be, but I think he's ready to go," she whispered. "You might want to get down here before too long."

Half of this conversation can be cut because it doesn't say much of anything. The weight of the phone call lies in the last couple of sentences, so that's the only part we need. Before you add in the niceties of conversation, make sure the exchange is going to accomplish a purpose.

Bite #62
Just Right, Goldilocks

Adding detail to your story is critical to making it interesting and informative. Adding detail to the dialogue you include in your story is equally critical, but it requires finesse. You definitely want to take advantage of dialogue to educate your reader, but you can't add so much that it sounds *written* rather than spoken. Read this to see what I mean:

"I love your bright red bonnet with the tiny white flowers and blue centers, Grandma," I said, seeing my grandmother's new hat for the first time.

"Mais chere, I bought this for $5 at Mr. Charlie's store in Charenton that's been on that same corner for fifty years," she said. "That's where I get my groceries each week. He has all kinds of things besides groceries."

Lots of good information in this exchange—a description of Grandma's hat and information about Mr. Charlie's store—but does it sound like a real conversation? I'm afraid not. When writing dialogue, we can't sacrifice believability to tell the reader things we think she might want to know. We need to find other methods and not take this easy way out.

Bite #63
Say What?

"Don't be late. *Tante* Marie made a king cake for the Mardi Gras *fais do-do* to go along with her *filé gumbo,* crawfish *étouffée,* catfish *courtbouillon* and big pot of chicken-andouille jambalaya," Alphonse told his buddy Cotton. "She threw in the cake as *lagniappe.*"

This is perfectly understandable to me, but if you're not from South Louisiana, you may need a translation. Alphonse is saying Aunt (*Tante*) Marie made a traditional, doughnut-shaped cake (*king cake*) for the street dance (*fais do-do*) at the Mardi Gras (a celebration that occurs the day before Lent begins) as a little extra (*lagniappe*) to go along with a type of browned-flour-based soup (*gumbo*) seasoned with powdered leaves from the sassafras tree (*filé*), a stew made with crawfish tails (*étouffée*), chunks of catfish in a spicy, tomato sauce (*courtboullion*) and a mixture of chicken and sausage (*andouille*) combined with onions, bell peppers and celery and white rice (*jambalaya*). Makes me hungry just thinking about it.

Bite #64
It's Greek to Me

You have to know your audience when you're writing dialogue. If I write this for my fellow Cajuns, nothing more is necessary. Most anyone else requires a translation. I like jargon, colloquial terms and sayings because they give an authentic feel to what's being said. Just be sure you don't leave your reader behind. The greatest technical, colloquial or occupational jargon is wasted on your reader if he can't follow what you're saying.

You can interpret what's being said for your reader in a number of ways. One is to write the definition of the unusual terms in parentheses following the word. For example:

> *Tante* Marie (Aunt Marie) said, "I made a king cake (a donut-shaped cake) as *lagniappe* (a little something extra)."

However, there are better ways to give the reader the information he needs to understand. Although correct, I believe putting definitions in parentheses breaks up the flow of the dialogue. This approach is better:

> *Tante* Marie, my mother's sister, said, "I made a king cake for *lagniappe*," as she handed me the donut-shaped cake, which she brought as a little something extra.

Here the unfamiliar words are being interpreted for the reader in a more casual way. The explanations are written right into the story, it sounds authentic and the flow is not interrupted in any way. *Comprends*? Understand?

Bite #65
Where Ya From?

Sometimes when I get excited, my Cajun dialect takes over, and people look at me in odd ways. I really am speaking English, only with a twist. Give your reader the flavor of the language as it is spoken by the people you're writing about.

Loyd, one of my students, is a self-proclaimed country boy from the Florida Panhandle, and his vocabulary contains quite a few words and phrases I've never come across. I first heard the term *pig trail road* from Loyd. In Louisiana, we call it a *double-track road*. Here are some of my favorite *Loydisms*:

tater pie—sweet potato pie
bellywasher—large drink or soda
cat-head biskits—large biscuits, the size of a cat's head
pig-trail road—small, unpaved country road
rollin' store—large truck or bus converted to a store stocked with groceries and other
     essentials that travels from house-to-house in rural areas
iffin—if you . . .

But again, don't overdo the dialect. Do not try to write every word in the tongue of the speaker. Pick out a few words to write as the person says them and use those consistently throughout your story.

Bite #66
I Know That

A cardinal rule in writing is don't use dialogue as a way to communicate information to the reader that the speakers already know. A reader can smell this kind of contrived writing a mile away and will know he's being manipulated. Read this to see what I mean:

"My husband Etienne, who has been a sugarcane farmer for thirty-five years, knew how
    to swing a cane knife before he learned how to cut his own pork chop with a table
    knife," Louise said. "Our daughter Grace, who now lives in the city of Lafayette
    with her husband Guillaume and her three-year-old son T'Frere, got so mad at
    Etienne for taking little T'Frere out to the cane field and showing him how to use a
    cane knife."
"I bet she did," Louise's best friend Rita said.

Okay, it doesn't take an Einstein to figure out if Rita is Louise's best friend, she likely knows Etienne is a sugarcane farmer, their daughter Grace is married with a young son and lives in Lafayette. All the background information is put in the dialogue only to fill in the reader. Don't do it. The only thing new is that Etienne let his three-year-old grandson use a cane knife, and it angered his daughter. Find other, better ways to get the reader what he needs to know to understand the current information.

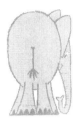

Bite #67
You're All Alike

Here's something to avoid. You don't want all the people in your story to sound alike when you write dialogue. This happens most when someone is *writing* dialogue and not attempting to make it sound like real speech. Yes, you are going to put in taglines that identify the speakers, but it's even better if the language and the sound of each person's voice have their own unique flavors. Say, for instance, I am writing a conversation between my crazy, Cajun cousin Louie and a Harvard law professor. If those two sound alike, I'm in trouble. My dialogue is not believable.

Try it out for yourself. Take two vastly different people in your world and make up a conversation just for fun. Do the two sound alike? If so, it's back to the computer or the pad of paper. Think about what makes the speech of each person unique. Word choice? Accent? Pronunciations? Topics of conversation? Gestures? Speech patterns? Sayings? Now rewrite your exchange and put in the uniqueness of each person. Sounds more authentic? I bet it does.

Bite #68
Build It Right, and They Will Read It

I've been putting off addressing this topic, but alas, the time is here. How the heck do you punctuate dialogue? Time to punt. Refer to Bite #187—In or Out? for the rules on quotation marks and where to put periods, commas, colons, semicolons, question marks and exclamation marks in dialogue.

Let me say this before I move on. There are many published memoirs out there where you cannot find a single pair of quotes even though dialogue abounds, and it works for them. I'm of the old school, and I don't suggest getting creative with any type of punctuation. Follow the basics of good grammar and save your creativity for telling the story.

Bite #69
A Long-Winded Speaker

General rules of dialogue suggest that your speaker does not go beyond three or four lines of speech without interruption by the author, adding in some background information, an action or inclusion of another speaker. *But*, there are exceptions to this rule.

If your speaker is long-winded and goes on and on and on, quoting him may well take more than one paragraph. In whatever way the situation presents itself, you do not want to put a closing quotation mark when the dialogue wraps to the next paragraph. For example, here's my friend Sara, telling me a funny story:

> A little, 97-year-old woman named Sara whose body is trying to fold in on itself told me a funny story as I stooped down to pet a local dog. She said, "One time I was in this hardware store, and the owner had a sign up that said, 'Beware of Dog.'
>
> "I looked around, and all I saw was this hound dog, sleeping on the floor under the sign. I asked the store owner, 'Hey, is that the dog I need to beware of? He doesn't look too scary to me.' The owner answered me, saying, 'Ma'am, I put the sign there, so people don't trip over him.'"
>
> "That's such a funny story," I said, laughing so hard it hurt.

I know a few dogs that would qualify for such a sign. You notice there are beginning quotation marks in each paragraph, but only the second paragraph contains an end quote mark as well. This is how it's punctuated when quoting a lengthy segment of speech.

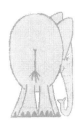

Bite #70
Kind of Like But Not Quite a Quotation

Many times instead of actually quoting a person, we paraphrase what he or she said. Usually you will see the word *that,* which alerts you that quotation marks are not really needed. For example:

I told Susan *that* I liked my daddy's boiled crawfish better than any other I've ever eaten.

No quotation marks are required, but if I change the sentence even a little bit, I need to drag out those quotation marks. Look at this sentence,

I told Susan, "I like my daddy's boiled crawfish better than any other I've ever eaten."

It's no longer a paraphrase; it's a direct quote, so put in those marks to let the reader know someone said something.

Bite #71
Capitalize That

To capitalize or not to capitalize, that is the question when writing dialogue. The answer is to capitalize the first word in every *complete* quotation. What do I mean by a complete quotation? It's one that is a fully formed sentence. For example, here's a complete quotation:

"*Nonc* T'Blanc grows potatoes in his garden," my dad told James. "He's done it every year since 1968."

You see, both parts of that quotation are sentences, so *nonc* and *he's* should be capitalized. If I change up the way this quotion is written, then the capitalization rules change as well. Look at this:

"*Nonc* T'Blanc grows potatoes in his garden," my dad told James, "and has done it every year since 1968."

This quotation says the same thing, but it's written in a slightly different way. The second portion of the quotation is a continuation of the first, so you capitalize *nonc* and use a lowercase *a* in *and*.

Bite #72
Commas and Attribution

We use commas to set off attribution when we are writing dialogue. Attribution is a four-syllable word that means giving credit where credit is due. We writer types call them taglines sometimes. Same thing. Look at the previous example:

"*Nonc* T'Blanc grows potatoes in his garden," my dad told James, "and has done so every year since 1968."

A comma after the first portion of the quotation creates a pause where we then learn who is speaking. Another comma is needed to separate the attribution from the second half of the quotation. This is true only when that which follows the tagline is not a complete sentence. When the second part is a full sentence, we use a period after the attribution, like so:

"*Nonc* T'Blanc grows potatoes in his garden," my dad told James. "He has done so every year since 1968."

Bite #73
Add a Little Spice to Your Story

You probably now know more about dialogue than you ever wanted to know, but sprinkling a little *talking* here and there throughout your stories spices it up better than cayenne pepper. Take a few minutes and write a piece which includes a longer conversation. You can do it; just write it one line at a time.

Bite #74
Take a Test Drive

Your dialogue is written. You think it's great. You applied the lessons learned in all the previous bites. You're ready to take it out for a spin. Always, always, read your dialogue aloud to hear how it sounds outside of your own head. You may be amazed that the way the conversation reads on paper is not at all how it meets the ear when your words become sound waves.

Usually, if you trip over a word or phrase, the reader will too. Sometimes things that make perfectly good sense when read silently are vague and confusing when read aloud. Even better, read your dialogue to an honest friend—not one who tells you everything you do is great; we all need those kinds of people but not for this exercise—and see what he or she thinks. Make changes as needed.

Anatomy of a Story

In this section, I'm going to put you to work. Get a few sheets of paper and a pen or turn on your computer, grab a cup of coffee or tea and settle into an area conducive to writing. Think about a story you want to write. Start off with a small event—one that doesn't involve decades of time, various settings or multitudes of people—maybe something like a fishing trip with a parent or grandparent. That's simple—one day, a couple of characters, one setting, a single goal. You ready? Let's get busy.

Bite #75
What's a Story?

Every story shares certain characteristics. Each has a *beginning*, a *middle* and an *end*. It has *characters*, and it's set in a particular *location*. Sometimes a life story is purely a recounting, but typically there's an issue to resolve—someone in it wants something, is in dispute with someone or something, is trying to avoid something and so forth. This is called *conflict* in writer circles.

Every story has a *plot*, another word for a sequence of events, and these actions often build *tension*. A story also has a *resolution*. It might not be a happy ending, or it may be there is no answer, but that is an ending in itself.

Using only a few sentences, write a summary of the story you want to tell. For example:

This story is about going fishing with Grandpa Luke at the Charenton Canal and wanting to catch a fish. A couple of times a fish took my bait or got off the line before I could pull him onto the bank. After two hours, I finally caught a five-pound catfish we brought home. My grandfather cleaned it and fried it up for supper.

Your turn. Write out a synopsis of your story. Once you've done that, let's look at the components of my story, so you can identify those in yours.

Beginning—going fishing with Grandpa
Characters—Grandpa and me
Location—Charenton Canal
Central issue/conflict—wanting to catch a fish
Tension—fish taking bait, getting off the line
Resolution—caught a catfish and ate it for supper

This little anecdote has all the necessary components to classify it as a story. I bet yours does, too. Let's examine these sections individually, but don't put that pen away yet. You're not finished writing.

Bite #76
Get the Hook

In the beginning of a story, you have the opportunity to capture the reader's attention, and you must if you want her to continue reading. We have so much information thrown at us daily, and our attention spans appear to be getting shorter all the time. Even if you're writing your personal or family history and the reader *should* be interested, you still have to give him a reason to read the next sentence and the next paragraph.

One way to capture a reader's interest is by using what is called a *hook*. The writing has to catch the reader's attention and entice him to go further. Think of a hook as something that causes you to stop and look when you're channel surfing. Likewise, we want the reader to stop and read our story. A hook can be many things. Maybe your story starts with action, which makes the reader unsure of what's going on, so he reads on. It could be a catchy phrase or one that raises a question. Maybe your hook is an unusual person or some interesting aspect of his or her character. A hook can be almost anything as long as it is interesting.

Here's a possible hook for my sample story:

"Don't pull too soon, Pat," Grandpa said. "Let him take it all the way to China."

This hook works on several levels. It starts the story in the middle of the action. The reader hears one of the characters speak and knows the story involves two people, Grandpa and Pat. It raises a question in the reader's mind, "Let him take *what* all the way to China"?

Or maybe my opening sets the stage for what is to come, like this:

The muddy water of the Charenton Canal moved slowly beneath my red and white, plastic bobber as I sat on an upturned bucket on the bayou's bank. Grandpa chuckled at how intently I stared at my fishing line, willing something to happen. It wasn't working.

Bite #77
Opening Up a Can of Worms

In addition to urging the person holding your book to read on, the opening of a story may also accomplish other goals. You can introduce one or more of the people or characters, as we call them here, in that first paragraph or two. Establish your main character early on; the reader needs to be invested in this person to keep reading.

Often times, the setting or location of the story is identified in the beginning, which may include a brief description and an indication of the significance of the place. This crucial beginning of your story can also jump right into the action and pull the reader along. Maybe your characters speak in the opening of your story, making the reader curious about who these people are and what they are talking about. Many ways exist to begin a story. Choose the best one for your tale. Now, write a rough draft of an opening paragraph, and then we'll move on.

Bite #78
Who Said That?

The people we write about tell our stories. As we discussed in an earlier section, characters should be more than simply names on a page. We need to turn them into real people whom the reader can hear, see and know.

First, list the names of all the people who will appear in this story. Then next to each name, write a couple of characteristics that identify them. You can weave these traits into your text as you write it. For example:

Grandpa Luke—quiet, grayish-brown hair, thin, always wore a hat, easygoing, long face, loved to fish, wire-rimmed glasses

Pat—skinny, short brown hair, blue eyes, talked a lot, lots of energy, loved being with Grandpa Luke

You can write a paragraph or two to describe someone, but most times, it works best if you feather in details about the person as the story progresses. Look back at the section on characterization for reminders on how to bring the people in your stories to life. Finish your list, and we'll talk about the ending next.

Bite #79
All's Well That Ends Well

The end? Why are we writing the end? You say, "I have many details to write before I get to the end." Yes, you do, and we'll get there, but for now, follow along with me. A story's ending contains a resolution, but it doesn't have to be a *happily ever after* ending. Sometimes the guy doesn't get the girl, the beloved pet dies and the fish aren't biting. At other times, the ending is another beginning, possibly the end of one phase of life and a new start. If you are still in search of answers, the story may end with a question.

I have a happy ending to my sample story—I catch a big fish and accomplish my goal to provide supper for my grandparents. Write out your ending. Mine might read like the following:

> Grandma hurried to the screened porch when she heard me yelling out the truck window. It took all my might and a little help from Grandpa to hold up my prize *goujon* for Grandma to see. She hugged me, fish and all. While Grandpa sharpened his fillet knife, Grandma went inside and put her fry pot on the stove.

Your turn. Write the ending of your story.

Bite #80
Set the Stage

Every story happens somewhere, so the area where your story takes place must be described to some extent. The location may play a big part in your story or be of no real consequence, but still some attention must be paid to giving your characters a place to do what they do.

Imagine a play in the theater. The actors are on the stage, reciting their lines, and all around them is the setting. Props are deliberately placed in certain areas. Painted backdrops depict the place and time in which the play is set. The audience's experience of the play would not have the same impact without the set. The same is true for your story, so take a little time and describe the setting.

Bite #81
The Place Where It All Happens

You have many ways to describe the location where your story takes place. There's always the physical description, but don't be satisfied with what can be seen. Think about smells, sounds and the feel of the place. What objects are there? What is the weather like? What's the season of the year? What is the locale's historical background? Are people part of the setting, e.g., crowds, street vendors? Are animals involved? What is the mood like? The lighting? All of these elements may be helpful in describing your setting.

Take a few minutes and make a list of the significant places in the story you're writing. Then write a few words to describe each place, for instance:

Sugarcane field—tall stalks of cane, double-track dirt road, sunshine

Inside my grandfather's truck—Ford, windows down, stuck to the vinyl seat in summer, tools in back

Charenton Canal—at the end of a sugarcane field road, muddy, slow moving

Bank of the canal—over grown with weeds, small area patted down, two or three-foot drop to the water

Okay, how did you do outlining the settings of your story? *Très bien.*

Bite #82
The Middle of the Road

If you followed instructions up to this point, you now have the beginning and ending of your story, a list of the characters and a rough sketch of the setting. Let's work on the middle, which is the largest portion of your story. The *plot* unfolds in this central section and usually contains the *conflict* or *main issue* of the story. *Tension* moves the story forward and keeps the reader interested.

Think through the sequence of events that brings you to the resolution at the end of your story. List each of those points. Here is what the plot line of my story might look like:

Ask Grandpa if we could go fishing

Dig for worms in the backyard

Load the truck with our cane poles and tackle box

Ride through the sugarcane field to the Charenton Canal

Set up on the bank of the bayou and bait our hooks

Sit quietly on an upturned bucket, watching the bobber

Get the first bite, pull too soon

Get second bite, fish takes the bait

Catch small catfish, too little to keep

Grandpa catches a couple nice-sized fish

Catch an eel

Get a hard hit on my line

Grandpa tells me what to do

Catch a five-pound, yellow catfish

Pack up our stuff and head home

Can't stop talking, so excited

Call to Grandma to come out and see my fish as soon as truck pulls into the driveway

Grandma takes a picture of me with my fish then puts a fry pot on the stove to heat

Bite #83
And the Title Goes To . . .

Now that you have a good sense of your story's design, it's time to give it a working title. I call it a *working* title because this is one to use while writing the story. When you're finished writing and editing your story, take a look at your title again. Maybe it's still the perfect introduction to the story you've written. If so, that's great; go with it. If you feel lukewarm about it, read on.

Titles of all kinds set out to accomplish a number of things. Primarily, they are written to catch the reader's attention. Even before the hook of your first paragraphs, the few words at the top of your page pull the reader into the story, push her away or worse, do not impact her at all. When titling your story, you want to arouse curiosity, raise questions in her mind, give her a reason to read further.

The name of your tale should tell *something* but not too much of what the story is about. You don't want to give away the resolution in the title. Why should the reader continue? She already knows the ending. But you do want the title to reflect the story's content. You wouldn't want to write an attention-grabbing title about a puppy when the focus of the story is a hurricane.

Each piece you write has a tone, a feel, an attitude to it. This is the voice you hear in your mind when you read; therefore, you want the tone of your title to match the feel of your story. You don't want to write a frivolous or light-hearted title when your story is about the death of a beloved uncle or create a grave and troubling title for a fun, happy tale. Let's look at some do's and don'ts in writing titles.

Bite #84
That's So Clever

Keep your title short. Have you ever seen these long, convoluted titles that reek of self-importance? Those kinds of titles make me put aside an otherwise good story. That's what you don't want to happen. Typically story titles consist of four or five words. Sometimes one or two words do the job.

Don't try to be too clever or too cutesy. It backfires on the author more times than not. Puns and plays on words can work, but if you're not really good at it, it can have the exact opposite effect of your intention. When I began writing, I thought I was oh so clever when I wrote twists-of-phrase titles and takes on well-known works. Now, when I come across one of those, I cringe. They sound like the amateur I was.

Use strong nouns and verbs in your titles. These words create a powerful impact in the body of the story. Why not use them in your title as well?

Bite #85
How To Write a Title

List a number of possible titles for you story, especially when working on your final title. Don't jot one down and go with it. Try several variations and then pick the one that works the best for your piece. Here are some title possibilities for the sample story we're talking about.

Try some of the following approaches. Pull a concrete image from the piece—something the reader can see, feel, hear, smell or touch:

Beneath the Muddy Brown Water

Describe a setting:

Down a Canefield Road
Charenton Canal

Include the main character's name in some fashion:

Adventures with Grandpa

Copy a phrase, repeated expression or a line of dialogue from your story as a title, like so:

All the Way to China

When I interviewed Doris to write her life story, I listened as she described moments from her past. As she neared the end of one thought, she always said, "But anyway . . ." as a transition to her next. I used *But Anyway . . .* as my working title and kept it because it was a phrase used throughout her story, and it so characterized her. As soon as her daughter read the title, she began to laugh and said, "Yep, that's my mom." These types of sayings or phrases can be quite effective in titling your story.

Think about the action of your story and try adding *ing* to a main verb:

Fishing With My Grandpa
Sitting on an Upturned Bucket

Pick a word or two that conveys the main idea of the story:

An Afternoon Goal
Mission Accomplished

Your turn. These are only a few of many approaches in writing a great title for your story. Try a few and see what works for you.

Bite #86
Show, Don't Tell

Before I close out this section, I want to talk with you about a writing device that helps bring your stories to life. You hear all the time in writing circles, *show don't tell*. This saying encourages writers to *show* the action of the story playing out on the page rather than merely *telling* or narrating the story. Clear as mud, right?

Telling involves summarizing, reflecting, lecturing and so forth. Showing gives the reader an insider's view and allows him or her to experience what is going on as well as reading about it. Think of showing as a little movie playing in the reader's mind.

Typically showing has a more powerful impact upon the reader than telling. What would you believe more strongly—my telling you a boulder is falling down the mountain or you actually looking up and seeing the giant rock heading your way? Yes, we all tend to trust more of what we see than what we're told.

Bite #87
A Fish Story

Using an example from my fishing story, here's the difference between showing and telling. Let me *tell* you about my afternoon:

> One day I went fishing with Grandpa Luke at the Charenton Canal, and after not getting any bites and losing my bait for several hours, I finally caught a five-pound, yellow catfish.

Or I can *show* you, like this:

> The hot, summer sun had already ducked behind the large, water oaks and left Grandpa and me sitting on upturned buckets on the shaded bank of Charenton Canal.
> My backside hurt, and I didn't have anything to show for the last several hours I had spent watching my red and white, plastic bobber drift in the muddy water.
> I had almost fallen asleep with the cane pole in my hands when a strong tug jerked me awake. I jumped up and said, "Grandpa, I got something," as I saw my bobber dragged beneath the surface.
> "Good, Pat. Don't pull it too fast, just wait," Grandpa said in a quiet, calm voice. "Let him take that bait all the way to China." After what seemed like an eternity, Grandpa said, "Now, Pat, now pull up to set the hook."
> I yanked the pole up just like he told me, and then the fun really began. The fish came up to the surface and splashed all around then dove back down to the bottom. I pulled up again, and the big yellow catfish jumped and twisted all around, trying to get off the hook, but I had him good. The fish and I repeated this little dance a few more times before he finally tired himself out. Grandpa grabbed the net and scooped him up.

"Ya got yourself a nice *goujon* there, Pat," Grandpa said with a broad smile. "Damn nice fish."

"How big is he, Grandpa?" I asked. "He's got to be at least a hundred pounds, don't you think?"

Grandpa Luke laughed, "Well, maybe not quite that big, but I bet he weighs at least five pounds. We'll put him on the scale when we get home."

"Let's go show Grandma," I said as Grandpa got my fish off the hook and put him in the bucket I was just sitting on. He never let me take a catfish off the line because it has a barb on its back fin, which hurt really bad if you don't know what you are doing and get poked.

We put the poles and the tackle box in the back of the truck, but I kept the fish up front in the cab with me and listened as he grunted all the way home.

Whether I tell you or show you, the bottom line is the same—I caught a five-pound catfish, but which account did you enjoy the most? Probably, the second version. Why? You likely felt you were part of the action, that you were watching the story unfold right in front of you. That's what makes *showing* so powerful.

Bite #88
When To Show and When To Tell

Showing is great, but you have to be realistic. If you *show* everything in your story, you'd never finish writing, plus a good part of it would be plain old boring. The issue becomes, when should I show and when should I tell? Great question.

Show the important parts and tell the rest. How's that for a direct answer? I chose to detail the portion of my story when I caught the fish. That's a key moment; it's what the story is all about. Remember how we listed all the parts which made up the middle of your story? Use that list to identify the sections you'd like to tell. From my list, I may create additional scenes from the following:

Dig for worms in the backyard

Call to Grandma to come out and see my fish as soon as truck pulls into the driveway

Grandma takes a picture of me with my fish then puts a fry pot on the stove to heat

From your list, pick out the points you want to turn into scenes.

Bite #89
Make a Scene

Let's look at what goes into writing a scene. We've talked about characters, setting, dialogue, conflict and tension, all the elements needed to create a scene, so if you want a refresher, go back and reread those bites.

A few final words . . . let the events of the scene unfold naturally. Put the reader in your place and allow him or her to live out your memory. In the example I wrote, I place the reader on the bank, falling asleep while sitting on the bucket with a hurting backside. Then the fish takes the bait, and the reader is hanging onto that cane pole.

Another key element in writing a scene is to incorporate dialogue. In this example, the reader hears both my and my grandfather's voices. The next scene written would include my grandmother's voice as well. Write action verbs and vivid nouns into all of your scenes. Look at some of the verbs in the example—*ducked, jerked, jumped, dragged, yanked, splashed, dove, twisted, grabbed, scooped.* All of these verbs show action, and the nouns are interesting as well—*buckets, backside, bobber, cane pole, catfish, goujon, barbs, fins.*

Add sensory details to your scene, not only what you see but also what is heard, felt, smelled and tasted. Appeals to the senses in the example include the feel of the hot sun, the jerk of the pole and the sound of the fish grunting.

Try your hand at it. Pick one element of your story and write it in scene. Remember to appeal to the senses, use action verbs, choose concrete nouns, use dialogue, set the stage and create a movie in the reader's mind.

Editing and Revising

I hate to disappoint you, but you're not really finished after you write the last word. Sorry. You see, *writing* is a process, not a singular effort. In writing, you first pre-write, which involves gathering information, maybe doing some research, interviewing people. Next you take the information you have and fashion a draft, not necessarily even a good draft. I love what bestselling author and professor Anne Lamott tells her students. She says we need to give ourselves permission to write "shitty first drafts," pardon my French. (I've never understood why people say that.)

Then after you have the story down on paper, you begin to revise and change sections to your liking. Lastly, you proofread your story for typos, missing words, grammatical errors and so forth. Let's spend a little time discussing the second half of the writing process—revising/editing and proofreading.

Bite #90
Don't Edit Too Soon

Writing and editing are two entirely different functions, and they use different parts of our brains. Writing is a creative activity; editing is a logical process, and they don't play well together. If you begin to edit before you've finished writing, you run the risk of shutting down the creative process. Resist the temptation to go back and change the misspelled word that has the red, zig-zagged line beneath it on the computer or in your imagination. Don't read over the paragraph you've just written to change a few things around. Stay away from fixing the grammatical error you see on the previous page. All of that can be done in the revision stage of writing.

Write the story at hand (not your entire life story) all the way through to the end. Get the beginning, middle and end down on paper before you go back and tweak it.

Bite #91
Get Ready To Revise

When revising, you should *always* have several books within easy reach—a dictionary, a thesaurus, a good, basic grammar book and this book, of course. If these reference books are not right at your fingertips, it's too tempting to tell yourself, "Oh, I'll go back and check the spelling of that word later," or "This word is good enough. So what if I've used it three times in this paragraph."

Dictionary—Get a dictionary you will use. You can have the best of the best, which gives you the origins of every word, its linguistic history and so much more, but if it weighs fifty pounds, I doubt you're going to carry it around with you. Buy a collegiate dictionary and use it. Don't rely on the spellchecker in your word processing program. You can also consult a variety of online dictionaries such as *www.dictionary.com*.

Thesaurus—When you need a different word to say what you mean, consult a good thesaurus that has an extensive selection of words and is quick and easy to use. Most word processing systems have a built-in thesaurus, but it's limited. There are many good online options as well, including *www.thesaurus.com*.

Grammar book—Looking at all the grammar books available is enough to give you a headache. Each one tells you it's the easiest, the best, the most complete, the most painless, whatever, but all have their benefits and their flaws. I've yet to find a single grammar book that works for me in every situation.

Words are my business, so I have a bookshelf full of these little gems. I don't recommend that for you. However, you definitely need to purchase a copy of *The Elements of Style* by William Strunk, Jr. and E.B. White. It's compact and filled with years of writing wisdom. You may end up needing more than this slim volume contains, but start with this and see how it works for you.

Bite #92
Don't Do It

Absolutely do not trust the grammar checkers in word processing packages. It will send you down the proverbial rabbit hole again and again. Look at what it says, but verify its recommendation in a grammar book before you do anything.

One step above the grammar check in word processing software is all the online grammar sites, each presenting itself as *the expert*. Don't believe it. Many good sites exist, Purdue's online writing lab (http://owl.english.purdue.edu) being one, but before you take what any site says as fact, make sure it's reputable. Stay with those websites hosted by universities or similar institutions.

Bite #93
Just the Facts, Ma'am

I don't know many people who have encyclopedias in their homes anymore. If they do, the books must be severely outdated. But you need some means to verify the facts in your stories.

You can go to the library or purchase some type of general knowledge book, which may contain much of what you're looking for. One fact book I have is *The New York Times Guide to Essential Knowledge: A Desk Reference for the Curious Mind*. In addition to being a good paperweight—it weighs almost five pounds—this book contains a wealth of facts in many different categories.

If you're looking for current information, the Internet is probably your best bet, but here again, make sure the site is reputable. You don't want to confirm information from what you later find out is a sixth grader's book report. Laugh, but it happens.

Several encyclopedias have online versions but most are fee based. A few allow you to see some information on the topic requested, but you have to be a subscriber to view the entire article. Wikipedia usually comes up on every search and contains a great deal of valuable information, but here again, know that what you find there is written by unpaid volunteers across the country and can be edited by anyone, including you and me. That's not to say Wikipedia is not a good resource. It is, but you may want to corroborate your findings on another site as well.

Bite #94
Time To Revise

After you have the story you wanted to write in black and white, now is the time to review it and make it even better. Many of my class members hate to revise. They want to write the story out and be done with it. Sorry, writing doesn't work that way. The revision process is crucial to the success of your story. This is where you make sure you are telling the story you want to tell.

Look at revision in this way: imagine you are good at woodworking, and you decide to build a coffee table. You have all the materials and the knowledge you need, so you cut the pieces of wood to size and nail and glue them together to make a table. There's your table. It's finished, right? You can put it on display right in front of your sofa.

I can hear your mate: "You're not about to put that rough, unfinished table in my house." Why not? The answer is, it needs more work. Now that it's built, it needs to be sanded and stained and sanded again, varnished and sanded again to make it smooth and beautiful to the eye.

Revision is to writing what staining, varnishing and sanding are to woodworking. When you complete the first draft of your piece, you have something that looks like a story, but it needs to be edited to round off the sharp edges, smooth over the rough spots and make it beautiful, just like the table.

"Well, how do I do that?" I thought you'd never ask.

Bite #95
Hold It Up to the Light

When you revise your story, you have to detach yourself from what you've written to a certain extent. Put some time between writing your story and revising it—a couple of hours minimum, a couple of days, even better. Then you can look at the text more objectively. As you read through, ask yourself some of the following questions:

- **What is the story about?** That sounds silly, but sometimes we don't actually tell the story we think we're telling. We need to have a clear understanding of what our intention is to make sure what we write is in line with our message.

- **Does each paragraph support the story?** We all go off on tangents, in our minds and on the page. Sometimes tangents are great things; they lead us to new stories we may not have thought to write about, but they might not belong in the story you're revising. Make sure each paragraph contributes to the story.

- **Is your title effective?** As we discussed in a previous bite, a title should reflect the content of the story and pique the reader's interest. Watch out for gimmicky titles, plays on words, those kinds of things. Sometimes we can be too clever for our own good.

- **Does the opening grab the attention of the reader?** Like the title, your opening sentences and paragraphs need to be written in a way that will entice the reader to keep going, to read the next paragraph and the next and so on.

- **Have you adequately described the people in your story?** Make sure you have described the people in your story well enough for a stranger to get a feel for them. You don't want the important characters in your life to be only names on the page.

- **Have you adequately described the place(s) where your story unfolds?** Every story takes place somewhere, so it's always a good idea to give your reader a sense of the site. It doesn't take a lot of description to paint in the background of your story.

Bite #96
You're Not Done Yet

You're doing great reviewing your story. Don't stop now. Here are a few more points to consider:

What is the central issue, conflict or problem of the story? Make sure the reader is clear on what is at the heart of the story you've written. We call it *conflict* and *tension*, but it does not have to be some big dramatic event. The central issue may be as simple as what Mom is going to cook for dinner.

Are your concrete facts correct? Big one. The key word here is *concrete*. This doesn't mean your memory of Grandma's apple pie has to match what Aunt Harriett remembers, but you want to insure the accuracy of verifiable information, e.g., dates, spellings of names and places, seasonal occurrences, public events, etc.

I remember my mother reading a book about South Louisiana where the author had certain flowers blooming at the wrong time of the year. I read right over it, but my mother is a gardener and knew this detail was not accurate. When you have a fact that's incorrect, believe me, someone will notice it and usually take great delight in telling you about your mistake. Bottom line—if it can be verified, do it. Don't needlessly undermine your credibility.

Well, if you haven't thrown the book across the room by now, you're serious about writing and want to tell an interesting and compelling story. Bravo! This is why most people don't like the revision process. It's not always easy, but the effort you put into revising your work will reap ten-fold results.

Bite #97
Check It Once, Twice, Maybe a Hundred Times

The last step in the writing process is proofreading. Here you look for grammatical mistakes, punctuation errors, misspelled words, missing words (my personal favorite), capitalization inconsistencies, etc. Many excellent tips exist to help keep your story error free. Here are a few:

Proofread your story one to three days after you finish it.

Read your story aloud in a slow and deliberate manner.

Proofread a printed copy. Don't rely on the computer screen alone.

Pay close attention to the *little* words—*or, of, it, is, for.* It's very easy to interchange these words.

Look for missing words. We often read right over absent little words. Like the anonymous author said, "Proofread carefully to see if you any words out."

Read your story backwards, right to left, to catch misspellings and typos.

Proofread one line at a time and use a sheet of paper to cover up the rest of the text.

Examine your verbs. Make sure they show action whenever possible.

Have someone else read your story, looking for mistakes. I once heard an author say she offered readers $5 for each mistake they found. I'm not sure my bank account could support that.

If you're writing on a computer, review the findings of the spellchecker. Don't automatically change everything it recommends, but take a look. The program often finds mistakes the writer misses.

Do everything you can to insure your stories are error free, but when all else fails, you may want to cover yourself, like I often do, with a blanket statement at the beginning of your book. On one of the front pages, I typically print, "All grammatical and typographical errors were intentionally placed in this book for your pleasure in finding them." Don't we all feel a little superior when we find someone else's mistakes?

Bite #98
Common Mistakes, Part I

You can find lists of common writing mistakes everywhere—in books, on the Internet, in any kind of writing guide available. I'm not going to spend a great deal of time restating what you can find elsewhere, so I encourage you to check out some of these compilations. They are extremely helpful in determining and remedying often-made mistakes. The following are some commons slip-ups I see:

it's—its
it's is a contraction for *it is*
its is a possessive pronoun
It's cold outside.
The dog wagged *its* tail.

who's—whose
who's is a contraction for *who is*
whose is a possessive pronoun
Who's going to the dance?
Whose coat is this?

you're—your
you're is a contraction for *you are*,
your is a possessive pronoun
You're late.
Take *your* hat and leave.

they're—their—there
they're is a contraction for *they are*
their is a possessive pronoun
there calls attention to or identifies a place
They're going home now.
This is *their* cat.

There is the car I want.

There is a snake next to that rock.

among—between

among indicates a relationship of three or more

between involves only two entities

He was *among* the six who made the team.

The runoff was *between* Russell and his brother.

that—who

Use *who* when writing about people, *that* with inanimate objects

I worked with Jackie *who* lives in Franklin.

I looked for the watch *that* I lost.

very, really, pretty, a little

All these words are qualifiers and are not needed. Here's what author Mark Twain has to say about *very*:

> "Substitute 'damn' every time you're inclined to write 'very'; your editor will delete it and the writing will be just as it should be."

1950s, 1800s, 1730s

You don't need an apostrophe when making a decade plural. The apostrophe makes it possessive.

The *1960s* was an interesting decade.

The *1960's* fashions are back in style.

Bite #99
Common Mistakes, Part II

Commit these to memory:

1—100

Spell out numbers less than 101

The *sixty-six* choir members sang at church.

The *ninety-nine* soldiers returned home.

We sent out *200* invitations to the party.

would

Would can be used to indicate habitual past behavior, but I find it is habitually
overused. Read your sentence using the past tense without the *would* and see if it
works. Removing *would* usually makes your sentence stronger.

Jim *would eat* cornbread every morning for breakfast.

Jim *ate* cornbread every morning for breakfast.

affect—effect

affect is *usually* a verb

effect is *usually* a noun

His card *affected* my mother. (verb)

His pleas had no *effect* on my father. (noun)

farther—further

farther refers to physical distance

further to additional time, amounts or abstract ideas

Her house is much *farther* away than I expected.

I don't want to discuss this issue any *further*.

bare—bear

bare can be an adjective or a verb

bear can be a noun or a verb

The *bare* walls made the room look stark.

He *bared* his soul.

The *bear* came right into our backyard.

He had to *bear* the weight alone.

Don't repeat the same words

We have lots of words at our disposal. There are roughly one million words found in
English language dictionaries, so we don't have to use and reuse the same ones
in the same or nearby sentences. Get a thesaurus and find some new words.
Sometimes, it's not possible but make an attempt to add variety to your writing.

Wrong: I saw David's new car, and it's a beauty. His car is bright red with tan interior, and it has that wonderful, new car smell. I'd love to drive that car!

Better: I saw David's sporty new *Corvette*, and it's a beauty. The *coupe* is bright red with tan interior, and it has that wonderful, new car smell. I'd love to drive that *baby*!

Bite #100
Know Thyself

We all have mistakes we make unconsciously, ones we need to become aware of to better edit our own work. When you notice you repeat the same error, write it down. Begin compiling a list of these oversights, so you can look for them specifically as you revise your story.

For example, I know better, but I repeatedly type *your* instead of *you* or put *ed* onto the end of a word when I need *ing*. No matter how much I will myself to not make these transpositions, I continue to find them in stories, emails, letters and most everything else I type. Interestingly, I don't make them when I handwrite, so it must be related to certain combinations of key strokes.

I finally started keeping a list of my *favorite* mistakes:

you and *your*	*out* and *our*
ed and *ing*	*than* and *that*
not and *now*	*ever* and *even*
for and *from*	*live* and *life*

Start making your own list, and as you come across other examples of unconscious errors, write them down. Then, as you edit, search out each instance of these troublesome words and confirm its accuracy. If you're using word processing software, you can easily locate each instance and repair the damage before your story gets in the hands of the reader. Making these mistakes won't get you thrown into the grammar dungeon, but they certainly undermine your credibility as a writer.

Bite #101
It's Just so Unjust

Just like we all have our favorite mistakes we make repeatedly, we usually have a handful of words we write into every other sentence. For me, it's *just*. My friend and fellow writer Elaine pointed out my affinity for the word, and until then, I hadn't realized *just* how much I use *just*. *Just* is a great word; it fits *just* about everywhere. Even Nike thinks so—*just* do it. A search for my four-lettered friend turned up way too many appearances, and I *just* had to thin them out.

Shortly after my *just* episode, I purchased a software program, which counts the instances of each word in the text. Wow! I found *just* had a few friends—*that, this, your*. So, I advise you to scrutinize your text and identify the words you include by default. Then make a list, and when you're finished writing a story, do a search of all instances of those words. Look at each occurrence, and if the sentence makes sense without it, cut it. Some words and phrases that may fit into this category include *that, very, really, kind of, like, quite*. Delete.

Bite #102
Missing You

Another thing I do often is leave words of a sentence. Did you get that? I just left out *out*. Sometimes our brains fill in the details, and we read right over those missing words, but we need to be diligent here because leaving out a word like *not* can drastically change the meaning.

A friend in the medical profession told me about test results she received which stated, *pulmonary embolism found in patient's lung*. The test had been done on Friday, and my friend was reviewing the report on Monday morning. Because she didn't receive immediate notification, she figured that all important word *no* had been left out. The radiologist confirmed her conclusion, thankfully for the patient. Moral of the story: little words matter.

I don't know of many good ways to identify missing words. Certainly having someone else read your story will unearth a few of them. Reading your piece aloud can also help locate those AWOL words. Some software packages, Adobe Acrobat Professional, for one, include a feature that translates text to voice, so you can sit and listen as your words are read to you. Granted it's in a funny, machine language, but if it catches only one of those truant words, it's worth it.

Bite #103
Cut and Paste

The cut and paste feature in most word processing software packages is a wonderful thing and makes editing so much easier. When I began working for a newspaper in 1971 as a *seasoned* fourteen-year-old reporter, cut and paste was literally that. We took out the scissors, trimmed away the excess on the typeset section of text and smeared gooey rubber cement all over the back. If we weren't all asphyxiated by the smell of the glue, we then positioned the article where we wanted it.

We can now do all of that electronically by highlighting sections of text and issuing commands to cut it from its current location and paste it in some other place within the text. That's wonderful, but any tool must be used properly, and I often find mistakes which are the result of improper cutting and pasting. Either I cut too many or too few words from the original section, and the sentence no longer makes sense, or I paste the new section into text without removing all the old words I should have. Bottom line . . . carefully read *both* the original and revised portions of text before moving on.

Bits and Pieces

You know how you end up with socks and no partners when all the laundry is done? Where do they go? A pair goes in, and a single comes out—one of the true mysteries of life. This section is a little like those uncoupled socks; the tips don't match anything else, but they are too important to toss out.

The following elephant bites tell you about clichés, reading, writer's block, places to write, what to do when you're finished writing, etc. Keep reading. Mark them as you go: trust me—you'll use the information.

Bite #104
Stop in the Middle

The first time someone told me to end each writing session in the middle of what I was working on, I thought he was crazy. Why should I stop in the middle? Isn't it better to finish the paragraph, chapter or story *before* I quit for the day? What if I can't remember where I was going in my story?

I reluctantly tried it, and to my surprise, this trick worked! I found stopping in the middle provided several unexpected benefits. I didn't want to forget where I was going, so I kept thinking about my story and ended up with many more facets of the tale than I had before. I also couldn't wait to get back to the page, so I made my next writing session a priority. Then when I sat down to write, there was no getting-warmed-up time necessary. I jumped right in because I knew where I was going—no running in place while looking for a direction.

Next time you're wrapping up your writing time, don't finish that paragraph or sentence, stop in the . . .

Bite #105
More Than/Over

Language is a dynamic, ever-changing entity. Many of the rules I learned in high school and college no longer apply. I remember my first-year journalism teacher, Professor Eddie Bohner, banging into our heads there is no such thing as a *new record*, that by its nature, if it's a record, it's new. Listen to any sportscast today, and you'll hear *new record* at least ten times. Sorry, Eddie.

We have many words and expressions in the English language, which are interchangeable or may be acceptable before long, so I hesitate mentioning them, but I'm going to anyway. I often see *over* used in place of *more than*. I was taught *over* means *above* and *more than* means *in excess of,* but look in any modern dictionary, and you'll see one of the definitions of *over* as *in excess of; more than.* Go figure.

> I can't pay *more* than five dollars for a dish.
> I won't pay *over* five dollars for a dish.

Eager and *anxious* are two more words, which not long ago designated totally opposite moods. *Eager* was excitable, a good thing, and *anxious* was something to be avoided because you didn't want to be full of mental distress. Now the dictionary lists *anxious* as *earnestly desirous* or *eager.* If you're a traditionalist, stay with the original definitions; if not, use whatever word you'd like.

Bite #106
She's as Pretty as a Picture a/k/a Cliché

If you've heard it before, don't use it. Period.

Bite #107
Be a Reader

One of my students, Loyd, writes wonderful stories about being a kid, growing up in the Florida Panhandle, and he reads published memoirs when I force it on him, but otherwise he tells me, "I have two books, and they are both all colored in."

I believe reading helps us become better writers. My husband Bob enjoys reading books after I do, because I circle all the words I don't know, look up the definitions and write them in the margins. I also highlight phrases and passages I appreciate and pencil in a variety of notes wherever I can fit them on the page. He often says he likes reading my comments more than the book. This is the way I was taught to read—get involved, ask questions, look for answers, examine what the author is doing.

If you're writing your life story, you probably want to read memoirs by other authors so you can see how they approach the task. You may also want to examine other historically correct books that are set in the area and/or era you are writing about. This is so helpful, especially if you're writing about your ancestors.

I've heard this admonition for years, but to be honest, I haven't consistently followed the suggestion to read books of all genres. I wanted to pass it on to you anyway because I have no doubt it would greatly benefit me if I did read widely. There are many great memoirs to read; I have a difficult time prying myself away to make time for fiction or poetry. In this instance, do as I say, not as I do.

Poetry helps with understanding the rhythm of sentences, brevity, imagery and symbolism. Well-written fiction assists in all aspects of memoir writing, because we are adopting writing devices novel and short story writers have been using forever—

description, dialogue, conflict and tension, plot line, characterization and many others. Pick up a book, any kind of book, and see what lessons await you.

Bite #108
Reasons To Not Write

We all have them—reasons why we absolutely *cannot* write. Most of our excuses are not even creative; they tend to be in the vein of *the dog ate my homework*. (That really did happen to me once.) We say:

> I don't have time. I'm too busy. I'll do it tomorrow. I can't think of a thing to write. My computer is broken. My pen ran out of ink. I can't find any paper. I lost my writing notebook. I'm no good at this. I can't remember anything. The cat died. The cat didn't die.

The first line of defense against these self-defeating thoughts is to recognize them for what they are—excuses. Granted we do have lives to live and responsibilities to tend to, but we all know when we are making excuses to get out of writing.

Writing is labeled a discipline for good reason. It takes discipline to write, and some of the most talented authors are the ones who have the most difficult time writing consistently. My graduate advisor told me the story of a student who showed up in her creative writing class one semester. When she read the first story he turned in, she realized he was a better writer than she. She asked herself, "What am I going to teach this guy?" As the class went on, she realized she could teach him how to *finish*. Even with all the talent he had, he lacked discipline, and without discipline, none of his stories ever reached the last line.

Bite #109
From the Mouth of a Pro

I remember a well-known and widely-published author, Bob Shacochis, telling me once that out of his group of fifteen who received their Masters of Fine Arts degrees from the

Iowa Writing Workshop, he was the only one writing for a living. He also said the group contained writers more talented than he, but what he had that the others apparently did not was discipline and perseverance. He kept putting pen to paper no matter what—rejections, writing around a fulltime job, sick kids, everything—and eventually he had the attention of a publisher.

For most people, writing is not their livelihood, so it's easy to put it off for a day or two or forever, but that tiny voice, calling us back to the page never goes away. I totally gave up writing for almost ten years, and undoubtedly, it was the worst decade of my life. I knew I was giving up on myself as well as the writing, and I used all sorts of vices, attempting to quiet that part of me. It didn't work. I found relief only when I returned to the page, and I haven't left it since.

We all have one *big* reason to not give in to our excuses. None of us like to admit it much less talk about it, but we aren't going to live forever. We think we have all the time in the world to finish our life stories, but I've seen otherwise. I'm sure you have, too. We don't have to start thinking morbidly, but we do need to remember we may not have all the time we think we do.

Enough said. Turn on the computer or take out your pen and paper and write.

Bite #110
Writer's Block

I hear people say they can't write; they have writer's block. Most of the time, I don't buy it. It's a convenient excuse. I do believe writer's block exists, but before I accept it as legitimate, you have to convince me you've written thousands and thousands of words consistently and successfully, and then *maybe* I'll sympathize with you.

Even genuine cases of writer's block are rarely terminal, and medicine does exist to counteract the symptoms. It's called *writing*! Writing no matter what. The only way through writer's block is to write your way out. If you consistently show up at the page, your chances of recovery are great. If you don't, your disease is fatal.

Many exercises and tricks exist to confront writer's block, and most of them involve writing. One of the most successful I've seen is to write whatever is in your head that day in a stream of consciousness style. If you get stuck and can think of nothing else to put on the paper, then repeat the last word you wrote over and over again. Eventually, your subconscious will get bored and throw you a bone, some little nugget you might be able to do something with. This was the beginning of my writing day a few weeks back:

> I'm tired; I need to go back to bed. I shouldn't have stayed up late watching *So You Think You Can Dance.* Kent was very cute though. I'm hungry. What do we have to eat in this house? Have to go to the grocery store today. Maybe I'll do that after my exercise class. I can't get the new dance routine in class. I'll ask Renee to show it to me again. Read any good books lately? Writing like this is so stupid. I can't see how this is ever going to work. My head hurts. I need some Tylenol. No, I have to make myself sit here until something happens. Gosh, I might turn eighty before then. Well, I do remember this one time when my grandfather took me fishing . . .

And then I'm off and running. Sometimes it's a matter of getting all my to-do lists, my worries, my insecurities and especially my expectations out of my head, so a memory or an idea can come in. If we come to our writing tables anticipating what we write will be great, we'll have trouble ever getting words on the page. It's too much pressure. Remember, author Anne Lamott gives us permission to write "shitty first drafts." When I allow myself that kind of latitude, I usually come up with something decent, and if not, I still enjoy my writing time. If my fingers are rigid, my teeth clenched and my eyes burning holes into the computer screen, it certainly isn't any fun, and chances are the writing won't be worth much. Let go. You can't write and be in control at the same time.

Bite #111
I'm Out of Control

Speaking of being out of control . . . sometimes the best way to get out of a drought is to do something different with your writing. Write in a new place. Write on paper with no lines. Write sideways on your paper. Write with a crayon or marker. Turn your computer monitor to black and write in the dark. That produces some interesting results; you can't edit as you go along. Write sitting on the floor or up on the counter. Write while you're walking. The action you take is not nearly as important as doing it. Sure, you may feel silly, but silly never killed anyone. Shake things up a bit and see what happens. You may be pleasantly surprised.

Bite #112
Come On Over to My Place, Baby

One year, I had a calendar that featured a different writer's working space every month. From the boathouse overlooking the ocean in North Brooklin, Maine where E.B. White penned his tales about the barnyard to the countertop where a woman whose name I can no longer remember sat, laptop in hand to the many other studies, desks, front porches and coffee shops, most writers create spaces conducive to writing.

I recently finished reading a book by famed author and teacher William Zinsser titled *Writing Places*, which tells much of his life story based on the places where he wrote—from the offices of the *Herald Tribune* in New York City to Branford College at Yale to a converted garage overlooking Long Island Sound to the last of his writing places in a business district at Lexington Avenue and 55th Street in New York City.

Most of us aren't fortunate enough to have a room we can dedicate solely to writing, but we probably have a corner or a chair or a table we can call our own. Having a dedicated writing space helps our creativity. It's somewhat like the writing rituals we talked about in the beginning of the book that let our minds know we are ready to write. Going to a specific space in our homes or in some other area accomplishes the same purpose. It notifies our creative selves that it's time to write.

In establishing a writing space, look for a place where you're comfortable but not too comfy; you don't want to fall asleep every time you go there. Surround yourself with things you love—books, music, encouraging words or phrases, photographs of family, whatever makes this area yours. And then, when it's time to write, go to your special place, take out your pad or turn on the computer and free all those memories, waiting to make an appearance.

Bite #113
Here, There and Everywhere

I am fortunate to have several writing spaces. When it's nice out, I go onto the screened-in back porch of our third-floor condo, which overlooks a large Central Florida lake. I put my laptop on a folding table I have out there and begin stringing words together while enjoying the outdoors.

When I need to work inside, I have a desk in an alcove in the dining room, which also looks out over the lake. On days when I am distracted by every little thing, I put myself in time-out at a desk in a second bedroom that has only one small window and absolutely no view. It's somewhat dark in this room; I call it the cave. For obvious reasons, I don't spend much time in there.

Having a laptop makes you mobile, so your writing space can be almost anywhere. Some days I go out onto the dock with a lawn chair or take up residence in a chaise lounge by the complex's pool. Be careful though, those places can be dangerous. Naps hang out around chaise lounge chairs bathed in warm sunshine, waiting for the ideal moment to attack. And on other days, I leave my home entirely and ask the muse to meet me at a little tea place down the street or at Starbucks or any number of other places.

Writing in other locations provides a different type of creative energy. It doesn't make a lot of sense, but sometimes when I'm really distracted, I go to a public place where there is a lot of activity surrounding me, and there I'm able to focus better. Go figure.

Bottom line—write, anywhere, anytime, anyplace. Just write.

Bite #114
Have a Fan

When you're ready for someone to read an early draft of a story, get a person who is supportive and encouraging. Everyone needs a fan, and this is the person you want to eye your work first. It's a vulnerable experience to allow others to read what you've written.

What if they don't like it? What if they don't like me anymore? What if they tell me I'm no writer? That's why you want a fan to take your story out for its test drive.

I have never read a story that did not have positive qualities, so when I speak with a new writer, that's my focus. Make sure the person you choose does likewise. Unfortunately, sometimes the people closest to us are not the ones best suited to the task. They will often tell you, "I remember that time, and that's *not* the way it happened." They say you got it all wrong, a certain story wasn't true. Here I reiterate what my buddy Loyd tells his critics, "Go write your own book. This is my memory and my story."

Bite #115
Don't Be Afraid of the Pain

Telling someone to not be afraid of the painful parts of their past and write about them anyway is easy to say, much more difficult to do. All of our lives include pain, and many life story writers tend to write about only the good parts. They don't want to make their readers sad or bring them down in any way. They want to paint a happy picture. When writers do this, I believe they are shortchanging their families and their readers.

Power resides in the pain. These strong emotions have an energy, which transfers mightily to the page. In my late twenties and thirties, I put my pen down and walked away from writing, and when I did, I gave up on myself and opened the door to a decade of painful years. Thankfully, with the help of friends who knew my heart's desire and a professor who encouraged me, I found my way back to the page.

For a long time, all I wrote about was the pain. It's a wonder my laptop didn't short out for all the tears falling onto the keyboard, but I wrote my way out. Once I had the pain in front of me in black and white, it no longer seemed quite as threatening, and I felt freed up inside to remember and write the many happy memories I had. Sometimes we have to write our way out of those darker times.

Bite #116
Get Real

Many of the people I work with want to present their best side to the reader. They want to look good on the page, and I don't blame them. It's human nature to want people to like and approve of us and what we do. But if you choose this approach, you are cheating your readers, especially your family members. The person reading your book knows you are an imperfect human being. When you share your failings as well, a connection happens.

Write about what you learned from the mistakes you made. You may keep a young family member from going down a similar path. Give them the benefit of what experience has taught you. Tell them about regrets you have, what you would love to do over again. Write about missed opportunities, what held you back from taking certain risks. We all have fears—detail yours and show how your fears impacted your life. Let your softer side show.

Bite #117
Don't Preach

I've given you permission to share lessons and experience, but do not preach. Nothing will turn away a reader faster than someone lecturing to them, telling them what they need to do and how to do it. Slam! Book shuts, and you are up on the shelf collecting dust.

I helped a gentleman named Ron write his life story for his children and grandchildren. He had all these wonderful tales to tell, and at the end of each, he wanted to put a lesson, the moral of the story. I told him to hold off on the lessons, and let's see how his writing unfolded.

For the first few months, he talked about these *lessons* each time we met. I tried to discourage him, saying if he wrote about himself in a clear and honest way, his readers would take their own lessons from his experiences. He didn't believe it for one minute, but he trusted me, and we continued to write and edit without a lesson ending each story.

By the time we finished his book, he was a believer. He let go of his desire to lecture and the concern that his family would not *get* what he so wanted them to know. They understood. He wrote this to me in a note a few months after he shared his book, "I have since had many great discussions with all my family which have been very emotional for me and it gave me chances to talk about values and principles learned." We all teach by example. Write by example as well.

Bite #118
Try This

Grab your pencil, and let's do a little drawing. *Groan.* I can't draw either, but you don't need artistic ability to do this exercise. Sketch the layout of the main street of your childhood town or neighborhood, your house with all the rooms and finally, your bedroom. Now go back to each drawing and fill in as much detail as possible, e.g., the names of the stores, homes where friends lived, furniture in the rooms. The more precise you make this plan, the more useful this tool will be for you.

As you lay out the map of these places, pay attention to the memories they trigger. Jot them down in your idea notebook as possible stories for future writing sessions. Keep this schematic handy, so you can refer to it whenever necessary. Include additional details to the diagram as you remember more about the places of your childhood.

Bite #119
Play It Again, Sam

As I said in the beginning of this book, there are as many ways to write life stories as there are people to write them. Likewise, other options in addition to writing do exist.

You can do an oral or video history where you speak into a recorder or camera about your life and memories, and there is nothing wrong with that approach.

But—and this is a big BUT—if you choose to go the oral or video history route, have the content transcribed. It may cost you a little time or a few bucks, but it is well worth the trouble. Technology is moving at such a fast pace that whatever means you choose to record your story today is likely to be obsolete within a few years.

Remember the eight-track cartridges of the late '60s and '70s? If you recorded your life story on an eight-track tape, you would have a difficult time listening to it now. All that great information sits lost inside a plastic container. When you get the recordings transcribed into text, you will always have it. It won't become outdated.

Having said that, I think combining *both* text and audio/video recordings is a great idea. When helping others to write their life stories, I always encourage them to do an audio/video introduction to their books. Nowadays, you can easily record a nice statement on a digital camera, transfer the file onto a CD and place it in a pocket at the front of your book. That way your children, grandchildren and even great-grandchildren you may never meet can see and hear you as well as read your words. Hopefully, the people who receive your book will see to it to keep your digital message updated to the latest technology.

Bite #120
Just a Few Scribbles

One of our most personal and identifying traits is our handwriting, so I strongly encourage you to include a handwriting sample in your story. You don't need beautiful, cursive letters and words flowing across the page. It just has to be *your* handwriting. That's what your family will recognize—the hand that wrote the grocery lists, signed their report cards, penned letters while they were away at college.

I suggest writing your dedication by hand. This is an extremely personal portion of your book. It is where you identify the people you're writing for and typically express some type of sentiment. Handwriting transfers emotion from the heart to the page better than any other means.

I have an old, bug-eaten ledger of my grandmother's that I treasure, mostly because it's written in her own hand. The content of the book doesn't matter to me nearly as much as seeing and being able to trace the letters of my grandmother's own handwriting. It makes her more alive to me than anything else, even photographs.

My grandmother used the ledger to track bingo winnings, house payments of $38.50 for the only home she and my grandfather ever owned and $10 monthly payments against a loan of $1,000. In the midst of the numbers, she recorded births and deaths, dates of hurricanes and hospitalizations and little gems like "bought my new dust mop—Aug 1968—extra mop without handle" and "started air condition July 25, 1966" and "put new curtain in my kitchen—April 20, 1968." This information alone is priceless, but to see it in my grandmother's handwriting makes it much more precious to me. Within the loopy *Bs*, *Ps* and *Rs*, I also recognize the origins of my mother's script.

Bite #121
Slay the Dragon

Ron, my client mentioned previously, tells wonderful stories. He knows how to bring people to life, create action, build up tension and deliver punch lines with the timing of a professional, *but* he hates to write, really hates it. Yet he finished the story of his life two years ago. This is how he did it.

A friend wanted him to write his story so much that he purchased a personal voice-recognition software program for him, in this case Dragon Naturally Speaking. After creating a voice profile, Ron was able to tell his stories into a microphone attached to his computer, which then translated his words into text. *Eureka*, you say. Not so quick. Voice recognition software is a good option, that's why I'm mentioning it here, but it's not the answer to all your problems.

Voice recognition software can't distinguish between similar-sounding words—*there, they're, their*—so a good bit of clean up is necessary after the fact. And even if you are a great storyteller like Ron, you will need to add in more detail because we speak in a way which is significantly different from the way we write. Ron used this software to capture the bulk of his story, made corrections and then sent the text to me for editing. That's how we wrote his book, all 50,000 plus words of it, so as a tool, voice recognition software can be a great help.

Bite #122
How Long Does the Story Have To Be?

I am asked this question frequently, just as I asked my professors when I started writing. I think it's a carryover from our high school days when our teachers required so many pages or so many words, and we suffered through the task.

I will answer you as my professors answered me: keep writing until you tell the story you want to tell, then stop. No magic number of words exists. Every story is different. Some take only a few paragraphs; others take many pages. You know your stories better than anyone, so when you run out of things to say, put your pen down and congratulate yourself. Then move on to the next one.

Bite #123
How Do I Know When I'm Finished?

If you wait until you *feel* like you're finished, you'll never key in that last period of the last sentence of the last paragraph of the last page. There is *always* something else to write, some other story to tell. That's why I tell clients and students to think in terms of volumes.

Once you get a number of stories together, have them printed and bound or put them in a notebook and distribute them to your family members. Then start writing volume two. I can't tell you how many people wait until they get a certain number of pages written or until they tell a group of stories, and they never finish. They lose interest before ever doing something with what they've written.

Combat this by giving yourself a deadline. Maybe you have a wedding anniversary coming up or a family reunion or a birthday. Maybe you pick a date at random as your cut off. The date doesn't matter; the fact you give yourself a deadline does. And stick to it! That's why using a future event works well.

My client Bill planned to give his book to his family at a reunion in April. To have his book ready, he had to finish writing by the end of January, giving me the month of February to edit and get it ready for printing. In March, we went to print, and he had the books ready a week or so in advance of the reunion. Deadlines work. Set one and work steadily toward it.

Bite #124
Now What?

Congratulations! You have your life story written and edited. Now what? Let's put it together like a real book. What do you think?

I format most of the books I write and help others to write in *Microsoft Word*. Word has its problems, but with a little knowledge and some patience, you can lay out a nice-looking book using it. Many types of desktop publishing programs exist, and you certainly can purchase one if you're up to learning how to use it, but for your purposes, I'm certain a word processing program will suffice.

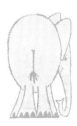

Bite #125
What Goes Where

Pick any book off the shelf in a library, a bookstore or your own bookcase, and you will see basically the same pages in the front and back of the book. It's not necessary, but you may want to pattern your life story manuscript in the same way. Here's a typical layout:

Title page—page containing *only* the name of your book

Copyright page—most life story authors do not actually register their manuscript with U.S. Copyright Office, but merely adding the copyright symbol, your name and the date of publication provides some protection. Plus it makes your book look official. The copyright page goes on the back side of the title page.

Acknowledgements page—this page exists for you to thank the people who played a part in the writing of your book—proofreaders, information sources, typists and especially those who encouraged you and made it possible for you to finish your project. You may also use this page to pay tribute to important people in your life.

Position your acknowledgements page either in the front of the book after the copyright page or at the end of the book, following the main text.

Dedication page—an inscription, an expression of thanks or a tribute to a person or a group of people.

Table of contents—a list of the individual stories in your book with corresponding page numbers.

Prologue, preface or introduction—an optional section which provides background information the actual text will not contain, introduces one or more characters, explains how you came to write this book, discusses your writing process or anything else that does not fit within the story line. Not all books include a prologue; the decision to do so is yours.

Epilogue or afterwards—this optional section provides information that extends beyond the end of the book. For example, you may conclude your book with the birth of your children. An epilogue might summarize your children's lives, detail the births of your grandchildren and so forth.

Timeline—an optional section designed to give a high-level view of a time period of your choice. The timeline may reflect the years covered in your book or may include extended family history. You can also restrict the items in the timeline to personal history or you may include historical events as well. Your timeline can be positioned either in the front or the back of the book.

"All this technical stuff makes the thought of writing a book way too complicated," you say. Understood, but you need not include any of these sections if you do not want to. Your book can be as simple or as involved as you'd like it to be. Some people want their life stories to look like *real* books. If that's you, browse through a few memoirs, decide what to include and go for it. If you don't want to be bothered, just write your stories and ignore this section altogether. Fair enough?

Bite #126
To Photo or Not Photo

All these choices. Okay, here's another one. Do you want to include photographs in your book? I believe you should. Without exception, when I hand someone a life history I've written, the first thing they look at are the pictures. Don't you do the same thing when a book includes photographs? I do. We love looking at snapshots even when we don't know the people.

To add photos to your book, you'll need to turn your actual snapshots into digital images currently called .jpg, .bmp, .tif or .png files. If you have a printer that scans, you can do this yourself, or take them to a copy center or some other store which offers photo services. Once you have digital files, then you can insert them into your text using word processing software.

Commander, Commanding Officer, Wing Executive and Wing Commander.

Dad's joy of being in the clouds continued, and his dream of flying a jet aircraft became reality in January 1955 when he flew solo in a T-33. He spent two weeks learning to fly jets at a Jet Aircraft Familiarity class at Craig Air Force Base near Selma, Alabama. The T-33 was a training jet, which all

Congrats and a handshake by Colonel Baines

MS Word and similar programs also have built-in features that allow you to do basic editing of your photographs—crop, brighten, adjust contrast and so forth.

Depending upon the word processing program you're using, you can be as fancy as you'd like. You can add frames around the photos, put in captions, change the shape of the images and so on, or you can keep them plain and simple. It's your choice.

Bite #127
A Real Book

What should you do with all these pages of stories and photographs? You know you want to give this collection of anecdotes to your children and grandchildren but how do you go about it?

You have lots of options here. What you do with the text from this point depends on how you want the finished product to look and how much you want to spend. I'll explain some options, tell you what to ask and then you can check with a local printer or copy center to determine costs and the best approach for you. Or you can ask your computer-whiz grandson to help or hire someone to handle all the technical aspects of your project.

The cheapest way to go is take your file or pages to a copy store like FedEx Kinko's, Sir Speedy, Office Depot, Staples or Office Max and have them print out the number of copies you'd like. Then put the pages into three-ring binders similar to what I suggested you use at the beginning of this book to organize your material. You can also print the copies yourself on your home printer, but depending upon how many copies you need, you may find you will spend more on paper and ink than you would at a copy center.

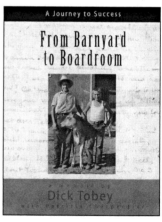

The next decision you'll need to make is how to bind the pages. One step up from a three-ring binder is to ask a copy center to spiral or comb-bind your book. For a little more money, you can ask for what is called a *perfect bind*. This style is the binding used with paperback books. Create a cover of some sort and give it and your text to the copy store or printer, and they will give you back a real book. I use perfect binding extensively with the clients I work for. It's reasonably priced and makes for an attractive, impressive-looking book.

Hardback or case binding, as it's also called, is certainly an option, but you will likely need to find a full-service printer to do this for you. Most copy centers do not provide this specialized service. You can have your book bound with a cloth or leather exterior. Or if you have a cover you've drawn or created with photographs, you may have this black and white or full-color image laminated onto a hardback cover, which creates a magnificent book. Of course, this type of binding is more expensive, so you may want to get a certain number of these printed for those closest to you and print the remainder by less costly means.

Whichever printing method you choose, make sure quality, acid-free paper is used. I'd hate to see you pour out your heart into this book simply to have the pages deteriorate within a few years.

The Stuff You Need to Know

If you've made it to this part of the book, you're serious about writing, and I commend you. But be forewarned, this section is not for the faint of heart or those prone to spontaneous naps. For most people grammar, style and punctuation discussions won't keep you up at night, flipping pages, but if you work your way through these additional elephant bites and apply what you find, your writing *will* improve. I guarantee it.

You can also use this section as a reference and revisit selected bites as you need them. Earmark those topics that always leave you scratching your head, wondering, "Now is it *lie* or *lay*," or "Do I need a comma before a conjunction," or "What the heck is a conjunction anyway?" Read on and find out.

Parts of Speech

Bite #128
Tools of the Trade

Every task has its own set of tools, and writing your personal history is no different. Our primary tools are words. We arrange them, shape them, polish them and display them in a multitude of different ways. We pick specific words to tell a happy story and other words to tell a painful story.

We understand one another because we have a *loose* set of shared guidelines of how to put these words together. I say *loose* because as soon as I tell you this is *the* rule about commas, you can find several examples from published, acclaimed authors who do otherwise. How we use words and punctuation is always evolving, but the question we have to ask ourselves is, "Does compliance with this convention make my story more easily understood?" This is our ultimate goal—to be understood.

Some people think it's so *creative, innovative* or *avant-guard* to set aside the principles of good grammar. I don't agree. I heard a famous author once explain she didn't use quotation marks because she didn't like the aesthetics of how they looked on the page. Okay, so when you're famous, maybe you can get away with stuff like that. But if you're like me and haven't sold millions of books, abiding by generally accepted rules of grammar is a good thing to do.

On the other hand, trying to make your story grammatically perfect is *not* possible.

Even the *experts* don't always agree, so don't cause yourself a lot of frustration pursuing an absolute, which doesn't exist.

With that said, here are a few basic rules of grammar and punctuation I believe will make your writing both interesting and understandable to your readers. I don't write this as an exhaustive style or grammar book; there are enough of those in print already. On the following pages, let's look at the primary parts of speech and learn how they can be used to improve your writing.

Bite #129
Nouns

Remember the definition of a noun from your grammar school days? A noun is a person, place, thing or idea. Many different types of nouns exist, but the main two are regular nouns and proper nouns. Proper nouns represent *specific* people, places or things, and by specific, I mean, it usually has a name. For instance,

> Washington, D.C., Acadia National Park and a beach of any sort are some of Joan's favorite places.

In this example, *Washington, D.C.* and *Acadia National Park* are capitalized because they are specific locations, places with names, but *beach* isn't because it's not a definite place. Joan likes any beach that has sand and waves; she's doesn't discriminate.

Bite #130
Momma, Daddy . . .

To capitalize or not capitalize . . . when should the woman who gave you life be *Mother* and when *mother*? This is often a troublesome issue in writing personal and family history. Those revered words like Mother, Father, Grandpa, Grandma and all the others are often capitalized when technically, they should not be. A way to remember this is to determine whether *mother* is a person's name or a label. For example:

"*Momma,* please fry some shrimp for dinner tonight," Belinda said.
Belinda asked her *momma* to fry shrimp for dinner tonight.

So, what's the difference between the two references to *Momma*? *C'est bon!* You're right; in the first example *Momma* is a specific person's name, the same as:

"*Eunice,* please fry some shrimp for dinner tonight," Belinda said.

In the second sentence, *momma* is not being used as a name; it is a title or position, an identifier or sorts. You can always tell whether to capitalize these words by determining if there is a possessive pronoun in front of the noun. When *his, her, our, my, your* or other possessives appear before a word like *mother*, do not capitalize it. The possessive makes it *not* someone's name.

One more time, if it's a name of a specific person, place, thing or idea, capitalize the noun; if it's not, let it be a regular, lowercased noun.

Bite #131
Pronouns

Pronouns are words that take the place of nouns, so we don't always have to call a person, place or thing by its proper name. You use them everyday: *I, me, my, mine, we, us, our, ours, you, your, yours, he, him, his, she, her, hers, it, its, they, them, their* and *theirs* among others. Without pronouns, reading quickly becomes tiresome. Keep reading to learn a few key points about pronouns.

Bite #132
Who Dat?

If you end up in New Orleans during football season, you'll likely hear, "Who dat say dey gonna beat dem Saints?" ringing out through the French Quarter. Everyone knows the *dey* (they) in this cheer refers to the opposing team. Whenever we use a pronoun, *we* know whom we're referring to, but the reader needs to know as well. Look at this example:

Joe and Jim are brothers, and *his* wife is Sally's sister.

Okay, we know Joe and Jim are brothers. That's great. And we know someone's wife is Sally's sister. Is it Joe's wife? Maybe. Could it be Jim's wife? Yes. Of course, I know Joe's wife is Sally's sister because I wrote the sentence, but the reader doesn't. The pronoun *his* is ambiguous in this instance. Put yourself in the reader's place and make sure the pronoun reference is clear.

Joe and Jim are brothers, and *Jim's* wife is Sally's sister.

Also, it's a good guideline to never begin a new paragraph with a pronoun. I know we have high expectations of our readers, but sometimes they forget from one paragraph to another whom we're talking about. Make it easy on them.

Bite #133
Make It Match

Just like nouns can be singular (boy, dog, race) or plural (boys, dogs, races), pronouns also stand for one or many. *I* becomes *we, he* becomes *they* when making pronouns plural.

The musicians took the stage, and *he* played *"Jolie Blonde."*

Here the pronoun doesn't agree with the noun it represents. The word *musicians* is plural, but the pronoun used, *he*, is singular. Make sure the pronoun you use to replace the noun matches in number.

The musicians took the stage, and *they* played *"Jolie Blonde."*

Bite #134
I Love It!

Long before Stephen King made *It* a sinister force in one of his many horror novels, that little, two-letter word confounded the likes of many. I love *it*. It's such a great word because it can be almost anything. It can be a goat or a table or a park or a job. It's an extremely versatile word, so versatile that it's often misused. Because *it* is such an adaptable word, we have to make it clear to the reader what *it* is. Look at this example:

Leroy caught a catfish, a bass and a perch. *It* was the largest fish he ever landed.

Old Leroy got himself a big fish. Way to go, Leroy. But was his monster the catfish or the bass? It probably wasn't the perch; a perch is a little fish, but you never know. It might have been a mutant perch. The reader is left with a question when a non-specific pronoun is used and not explained. In this instance, it's probably better *not* to use a pronoun.

Leroy caught a catfish, a bass and a perch. That *catfish* was the largest fish he ever landed.

Bite #135
Who Do You Think You Are?

Who and *whom* are pronouns and two of the most troublesome words for writers. At times, I still find myself writing around them. I've read so many tricks that swear they make using *who* and *whom* correctly a snap. Yeah, right.

Here's the deal—*who* is used to replace the subject of a subordinate clause (a fancy term for a sentence within the sentence), and *whom* is used to replace the object. Simple, right? Easier to say the rule than to apply it. The best way to decide if the sentence calls for *who* or *whom* is to substitute *he* or *him* or *she* or *her* for *who* or *whom*. If *he/she* works, use *who*. If *him/her* fits, use *whom*. For example:

Leroy is the man *who* caught the biggest fish.

Who caught the biggest fish is the subordinate clause. *He* caught the biggest fish makes sense, not *him* caught the biggest fish, so the correct pronoun is *who*. Now this one:

Leroy is the friend *whom* I enjoy fishing with the most.

I enjoy fishing with *him,* not *he,* so *whom* is the correct choice. Does that make sense? If not, write around those two little words and get on with your story.

Bite #136
Verbs Are Our Friends

A verb is the part of speech that makes or breaks our stories. Dynamic verbs make for dynamic stories. Dull, passive verbs put readers to sleep. You might have a great story and know all about good grammar and punctuation, but if you choose tired, worn-out verbs, your book collects dust on the bottom shelf. What are these *good* verbs?

Bite #137
What Is a Verb Anyway?

A verb is a part of speech that shows action *(jump, run, dive, swim)* or expresses a state of being *(is, am, are)*.

Antoine *jumps* on the couch.
Antoine *is* misbehaving.

Jumps is the verb in the first example, and it shows action. The verb in the second example, *is*, conveys Antoine's state of being; he's in a state of misbehavior, making *is* a state of being verb.

Bite #138
Make Those Verbs Sing

Verbs have a voice. Did you know that? In fact, they have two voices—*active* and *passive*. I guess it's like a vocalist who can sing both alto and soprano. I'm not trying to be your ninth-grade English teacher, but knowing this will help you write more compelling stories.

With active verbs, the subject of the verb is performing the action. With passive verbs, the subject of the verb is receiving the action. Clear as *gumbo*, right? Okay, see if this helps:

The dog *bit* Antoine.

Here the dog is performing the action. He bit the poor kid. (Bad dog. Where's the Dog Whisperer when you need him?) So, the verb *bit* is active.

Antoine *was bitten* by the dog.

In this example, the subject of the sentence, the *boy*, is receiving the action. He didn't bite the dog, so that makes the verb passive. Does this help?

Bite #139
To Be or Not To Be

A verb used in the passive voice where the subject is the *receiver* rather than the *doer* of the action often consists of a form of *to be* plus another verb. They usually contain one of the following words: *is, am, are, was, were, be, being, been* plus another word, which on a good day, could be a verb in its own right. For example:

Joseph *called* Marie on Friday.
Marie *was called* by Joseph on Friday.

You see the use of *was* plus *called*? That's the first sign this is a passive sentence. The verdict is confirmed when you realize the receiver of the action, *Marie,* is now the subject of the sentence.

Too many times, I see students struggle, trying to get passive verbs to do the work of active verbs. My advice? Look over your story and circle every *is, am, are, was, were, be, being, been* and see if you can change the sentences around to eliminate the passive verbs. Most of the time changing the verb in the sentence from passive to active involves flipping the sentence around. Here's a passive sentence:

The grass was cut by *Clarence.*

It is made active by reversing the order of the sentence and putting the performer of the action as the subject, like so:

Clarence cut the grass.

Bite #140
What's Wrong with Being Passive?

Nothing, if the passive voice is used properly. However, many times it is not.

You know when you go to a ballgame or some other event, and you end up eating too many hotdogs and feel sick? The hotdogs are not the problem—it's the over-indulgence that causes a problem. Same with passive verbs. A passive verb here and there is fine. At times, it's even necessary. But if you use passive verbs in each sentence, then the verb police will come out and round you up.

The ball *was caught* by my German shepherd puppy Lil Bit as he played and splashed at the edge of the bayou. The alligator in the water lilies *was not noticed* by Lil Bit. Finally the alligator *was sighted* by the puppy, just as *he was almost grabbed* by the beast.

Boring.

I *tossed* the ball to my German shepherd puppy named Lil Bit as he played and splashed at the edge of the bayou. With his eyes fixed on the ball, he *did not notice* the alligator that *lurked* in the water lilies. The beast *lunged* toward my puppy and *snapped* his jaws shut just as Lil Bit *yelped* and *jumped* into my arms.

Better, more interesting, don't you think?

Bite #141
When To Reach for the Passive Voice

Choose the passive voice when you want to show the subject of the sentence receiving the action. For example, when someone is victimized, you may want to show them as such. For example:

The woman *was stabbed* by the intruder.

In this sentence, I wanted to emphasize the woman in the sentence and not call added attention to the assailant, so I consciously wrote it in the passive voice. That's the key with this and all writing: make sure the choice you make to use the passive voice is deliberate. Here I intentionally chose a passive verb and had a specific reason for doing so; however, you do not want to get into the habit of writing in the passive voice.

Bite #142
I Feel So Tense

I'm spending more time on verbs in this book than any other topic. That should tell you how important these little critters are. Bear with me.

The basic verb tenses are present, past and future.

I *swim* in the bayou.

I *swam* in the bayou.

I will *swim* in the bayou.

The experts say there are as few as six or as many as thirty different tenses, but we'll focus on the three biggies—present, past and future. You choose your verb based on the time frame of action. It's either happening now or in the past or in the future.

Writers get into trouble with tenses when they change from past to present to future, back to present then past and go all around again. Try to use the same tense as much as possible. In recording our life stories, we usually write in the past tense because most of the events happened before the current day and time.

At times, we do need to dip into a different tense. We may say, "I remember one time when . . ." (present) or "This summer, I will visit the original home . . ." (future). But do so deliberately. There's that word again. Be aware, be conscious of the writing choices you make.

Bite #143
English Can be Challenging

For many reasons, I feel grateful to have been born in the United States of America. One big reason is I didn't have to learn English as a second language. I'm not sure I could have done it. I'd love to know who made up some of these grammar rules. Many times, the dictates of the English language are just plain aggravating.

Here's one of my personal favorites: when to use *lie* and when to use *lay*. Rule makers say we need to use *lie* when we are referring to an animate object, something living. On the other hand, *lay* should be our choice when we're writing about an inanimate object like a pencil or pen or sheet of paper.

Okay, I can live with that, but then it really gets hairy because *lay* is the past tense of *lie*. Don't you think the language experts could have found a different word instead of recycling the same one for an entirely different purpose? Like my Cajun grandmother always said, *Mon Dieu!*

I used to avoid *lie* and *lay* words for fear of making a mistake and looking stupid, but they really are good words. I had to come up with a way to feel confident I was using them correctly, so now I write out the present, past and past participle of both words and then pick the one I need, like so:

lie, lay, lain (to recline)

I *lie* down. (present)

I *lay* down. (past)

I *have lain* down. (past participle)

lay, laid, laid (to place)

I *lay* the pen down. (present)

I *laid* the pen down. (past)

I *have laid* the pen down. (past participle)

Sometimes I think English language gurus must have been bored when making up all this stuff because there are so many troublesome words in our language: *affect* and *effect, there, their* and *they're, its* and *it's, here* and *hear, principal* and *principle, farther* and *further.* Need I go on?

Bite #144
Adverbs

Adverbs are words that primarily modify verbs, as you might expect by the name. Adverbs have a place in writing and can be extremely helpful in describing *how* something is done, but overuse of adverbs weakens your writing.

The coonhound *constantly* chased the cat.

The adverb, *constantly,* describes how the dog chased the cat. This isn't a once-in-a-while thing. It's an ongoing sport for the dog. He must think the cat is a raccoon. To watch for adverbs, look for the *ly* ending. Most, but not all, adverbs end in *ly.* For now know what they are and what they do. In a future bite, we'll discuss how to avoid over-reliance on adverbs. Stay tuned.

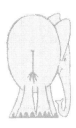

Bite #145
Adjectives

Adjectives are words that describe nouns—people, places, things and abstract ideas. Well-chosen adjectives add a great deal to the reader's understanding.

> *Grandpa's large, gray and white* coonhound chased the cat.

The adjectives in that sentence give us a better picture of the dog. We know the dog belongs to Grandpa. We also know his size and his color; he's *large* and has *gray and white* fur. But this description is still somewhat vague. How big is *large*—five pounds, ten pounds, twenty pounds? What's the design of the gray and white fur? Is he gray in the front and white in the back? Checkered? What if we write:

> Grandpa's *forty-pound, spotted, gray and white* coonhound chased the cat.

Now we have a clearer picture of the pooch. An adjective is one gizmo in your writing toolbox, but just like needle-nose pliers or a crescent wrench, it's not suited for every job. We'll talk more in a later bite about how to write description without solely relying on adjectives.

Bite #146
Handle With Care

A compound adjective contains two or more words, which work together to modify the same noun, and requires special handing. These multiple adjectives may be linked with a comma or a hyphen, depending upon how they are used. Boy, that sure clears everything up. Sometimes grammar is more difficult to describe than it is to use.

Here's the trick. If you can put *and* between the two adjectives and the sentence still makes sense, use a comma, like so:

Janice proved to be a *faithful, loving* wife to her husband.
Janice proved to be a *faithful and loving* wife to her husband.

The sentence makes sense with the adjectives separated by *and*, so use a comma between *faithful* and *loving*. When the *and* trick does not work, and the two or more adjectives combine to form a single unit, connect them with hyphens.

I learned to tie my shoes from my *left-handed* mother.

To say *my left and handed mother* does not make sense, so use a hyphen instead of a comma. Both of these rules work only when the adjectives are in front of the noun. When they follow the noun, no commas or hyphens are needed.

Roxy was a *well-trained* hunting dog.
Roxy was a hunting dog that was *well trained*.

All these rules may discourage you from using adjectives, which might not be a bad thing. Mark Twain has strong words for the lowly adjective:

"As to the Adjective: When in doubt, strike it out."
"When you catch an adjective, kill it. No, I don't mean utterly, but kill most of them— then the rest will be valuable. They weaken when they are close together. They give strength when they are wide apart."

Thanks, Mr. Twain, I'll be moving on now.

Bite #147
Hook 'em Up

Mostly, conjunctions are little words—*and, but, so, or, for, nor, yet*—to name a few. The conjunction is used to connect words, phrases or clauses. It's like a hinge. The hinge connects the door to the frame, which allows it to open and shut. The conjunction unites different parts of a sentence to create meaning. That's all I'm going to say about conjunctions for now. Later in the book we'll take a look at punctuation with conjunctions.

Bite #148
That's Prepositional!

Like conjunctions, prepositions are words that connect as well, but prepositions connect or relate a noun or pronoun to other words in the sentence. Often they answer questions of *who, what, where, when, why* and *how.* The most common prepositions include *about, after, as, at, before, below, between, beyond, by, for, in, like, near, of, for, on, over, since, to, toward, upon, with* and so on. Usually prepositions lead off a phrase, such as:

> Kelly went home *after the party.* (Answers *when* he went home.)
> The boy hid *in the bushes.* (Answers *where* he hid.)
> She spent the weekend *with her sister.* (Answers *whom* she was with.)

I remember being told over and over, "Do not end a sentence with a preposition." When I was in school, that was the crime of the century. I don't ever remember w*hy* ending a sentence with a preposition was so wrong—it just was. But guess what? Sorry, Miss Gilbert, we can now end a sentence with a preposition and not fear the red pen. I've even found it written in grammar books.

> What did he do that *for*?
> What did you step *on*?

These sentences are perfectly acceptable. To avoid ending a sentence with a preposition, we had to write convoluted sentences such as:

> *For what* reason did he do that?
> *On what* did you step?

Give me a break. The last two constructions make the sentences so much more formal than is intended.

Bite #149
Where Ya At?

As always, English has exceptions to its okay-to-end-a-sentence-with-a-preposition rule. Good grammar suggests when you can omit the preposition and the sentence still makes sense, drop it. The most notorious violation of this rule is using *at* at the end of the sentence, like this:

> Here's where it's *at*.
> Where are you *at*?

> In both examples, the *at* is not needed. Each sentence reads correctly as:

> Here's where it is.
> Where are you?

Bite #150
May I Interject?

The last part of speech is the interjection, and it's an easy one. *Oh my! Bravo! Wow!* As you may have guessed, an interjection is usually a little word that expresses a strong emotion. The word *interjection* means, "something thrown in" in Latin, so authors throw them in every so often, like:

Darn! The dog got out again.
Hey, what are you doing?
Boo! I scared you.

Caution #1: Write emotion into your stories. Show the sentiment and don't rely on interjections to convey strong feelings.

Caution #2: Using an interjection is fine here and there, but like I say about many things, overuse gets tiring to read. Your text starts to look and sound like the old comic books—*Pow! Bam! Zowee! Kapow! Whamm!* Holy interjections, Batman, one *bonk* goes a long way!

Sentences 101

Okay, you know what nouns, pronouns, verbs, adverbs and adjectives are. It's time to dig in, get our hands dirty.

Bite #151
A Basic Sentence

For a group of words to be a sentence, you need two things—a subject and a verb. You have to have both.

Etienne sang.

Etienne is the subject, and *sang* is the verb. Sentence complete. You're done. However, just to make things confusing, grammar rules say your subject can be *implied* and not written, as in the example: "Go!" The *you* is implied, and that's all I'm going to say about that.

Bite #152
Jazz Up Your Sentences

Yes, a subject and a verb are all you need to write a sentence, but reading gets pretty boring if that's all you have. Many adornments can be added to this basic sentence to jazz it up. Like a woman dressing to go out on a date, she can put on a little, black dress and look nice, or she can wear earrings, a necklace, bracelet, makeup, high heels, a hat, perfume and other decorations and be stunning. Adding objects, clauses, phrases, modifiers, punctuation and so on to your sentences accomplishes the same thing.

Okay, don't get all shaky inside; I promised you . . . I'm not taking you back to the ninth grade. You do not need to know the proper names for everything you might add to a sentence. It's nice if you do, but it's not necessary. Let's take a look at a few options.

Bite #153
Grab Me That Whachamacallit

An *object*, suffice it to say, is a noun or pronoun usually tacked on after a word which is somehow related to the verb. Boy, that really clears it up. It's easier to write an object than it is to explain it.

Etienne sang a *song.*

Song is the object of the verb *sang.* See what I mean? You write objects every day. Objects answer the question, *what* or *whom.*

An object can also come after a preposition as well as other constructions:

Etienne sang a song at the *festival.*

Here *festival* is the object of the preposition *at.* Enough said, moving on.

Bite #154
Modifiers

We talked briefly about adjectives (words that describe nouns—people, places and things) and adverbs (words that most often describe verbs). Both adjectives and adverbs are called *modifiers* and serve to make the noun or verb more specific. Well-chosen adjectives and adverbs add a great deal to the reader's understanding, but they become laborious if overused. Take a look at this:

Young Etienne sang.

Now we have a little more information about Etienne. He's *young*. This is still vague. Young to an eight-year-old and young to an eighty-year-old are two entirely different things. If you string too many adjectives together, your sentence quickly becomes overwritten:

Young, buck-toothed, foul-smelling Etienne sang.

Well, that definitely helps us picture this person, but it's cumbersome to get through. Bottom line . . . like a screwdriver or vice grips, an adjective is one gadget in your writing toolbox, but not every job requires it. Refer to the Detail and Description section for more on how to write description without resorting to adjectives.

Bite #155
Modifiers, Part II

Adverbs are also modifiers, which tell us more about *how, when, where or why* something is done.

Etienne sang *slowly*.

Like adjectives, adverbs should not be overused.

Etienne sang *slowly, methodically, gracefully* and *beautifully.*

Yikes! That's way over the top. By the time the reader gets to the *gracefully,* she may be comatose.

Most, but not all, adverbs end in *ly,* so if you see too many of these guys scattered throughout your story, *kill 'em.* Look back to Bite #31 where we discussed ways to avoid using adverbs to describe action.

Bite #156
It's a Phrase I'm Going Through

Something else you can add to your sentences to jazz them up is a *phrase.* A phrase is a group of words which work together as a single unit. Many kinds of phrases exist, but for our purposes, you only need to know a phrase is a group of words that cannot stand alone as a sentence.

Etienne sang a song *for his mother.*

The words *for his mother* combine to form a phrase. It's a phrase because *for his mother* does not have a subject and a verb. It cannot stand alone as a sentence; that's what makes it a phrase. *C'est tout!*

Bite #157
Santa Clause?

No, no, not the big, red guy that comes in December. A clause is like a phrase in that it is a group of words working together as a single unit. It differs from a phrase because it has a subject and a verb and can usually stand alone as a complete sentence.

Etienne sang a song, and *he played the fiddle.*

The second clause in this sentence is *he played the fiddle.* It's a clause because it has a subject, *he,* and a verb, *played.*

Bite #158
It's So Needy

I have a friend who had a Jack Russell terrier named Janie, and that dog was the neediest animal I have ever seen in my life. She'd meet me, or anyone else coming through the door—friend, repairman, burglar—on her hind legs, begging to be picked up and petted. To get any peace, you had to have a hand on her constantly.

I think of poor, little Janie when I talk about dependent clauses, clauses that need to be attached to something else to survive. Dependent clauses have a subject and a verb, but they cannot stand alone; they need to be *touching* other words. They do not express a complete thought. Remember the previous example of a clause that could stand on its own?

Etienne sang a song, and *he played the fiddle.*

If I write it this way, the sentence now has a dependent clause:

While he played the fiddle, Etienne sang a song.

While he played the fiddle is a clause because *he* is the subject and *played* is the verb, but it doesn't make any sense without another thought. *While he played the fiddle,* what? The thought is incomplete, which makes it a dependent clause.

In the next section, we'll discuss how to punctuate introductory clauses.

Bite #159
One More Time . . .

Here's a review of what makes up a sentence:

> *Etienne sang.* (subject/verb)
> Etienne sang a *song.* (subject/verb/*object*)
> Etienne sang a song *for his mother.* (subject/verb/object/*phrase*)
> Etienne sang a song, and *he played the fiddle.*
>   (subject/verb/object/*independent clause*)
> *While he played the fiddle,* Etienne sang a song.
>   (*dependent clause*/subject/verb/object)
> While he played the fiddle, *young* Etienne sang a song.
>   (dependent clause/*adjective*/subject/verb/object)
> While he played the fiddle, young Etienne *soulfully* sang a sad song.
>   (dependent clause/adjective/subject/*adverb*/verb/adjective/object)

Okay, I'm done. This is beginning to remind me of diagramming sentences, which still gives me nightmares.

Bite #160
It's So Complex

Now you know what a sentence is and all the *things* you can put into it to jazz it up. Your sentence can be one of four types, depending upon how you combine dependent and independent clauses. A *simple* sentence is just that, simple—one independent clause, comprised of a subject and a verb.

> Her *father drove* the wagon.

A compound sentence contains two or more independent clauses joined either by a conjunction—*and, or, but, so, yet*—or a semicolon. You'll learn more about semicolons in the next section.

Her father drove the wagon, *and* her brother walked alongside.
Her father drove the wagon; her brother walked alongside.

The thing to remember about compound sentences is that the two parts have to be closely related. For example, you wouldn't write:

Her father drove the wagon, and the hen laid two eggs.

Huh? Your reader will be left scratching his head and wondering where the chicken came from.

Next in line is the *complex* sentence. A complex sentence is made up of one independent clause and one or more dependent clauses, like so:

Even though he was tired, her father drove the wagon.

The beginning of the sentence, *Even though he was tired,* has a subject and verb, but it does not express a complete thought, making it a dependent clause.

As you may have already guessed, the fourth type of sentence is a *compound-complex* sentence, and it combines two or more independent clauses and at least one dependent clause. A compound-complex sentence looks like this:

Even though he was tired, her father drove the wagon, and her brother walked alongside.

Bite #161
Compound, Complex, Who Cares?

All writers, that's who! "Vary your sentence structure" is the writer's creed, and to fulfill that edict, you need to know the different types of sentences. Without a mixture of simple, compound, complex and compound-complex sentences, your reader will be comatose in less than fifteen minutes, lured into unconsciousness by sheer boredom.

We all have favorite sentence structures. We may not even know we're doing it, but we tend to repeat the format. When we do this, it becomes boring to read, even monotonous. You have many options available in your writer's toolbox, so make use of all of them, even that funny-looking *thingamajig* way down at the bottom you never quite figured out what to do with.

Pick up something you've written recently or sit and write a paragraph or two. Review this piece and mark the different types of sentences. What's the verdict? Are your sentences varied enough to satisfy the sentence-structure police? *Ca c'est bon.*

Bite #162
Slow, Slow, Quick, Quick

My husband and I love to dance. We've taken a few lessons here and there, and I find writing sentences to be much like dancing. You learn the basic steps the first night and then spend a lifetime discovering new moves and perfecting the old ones. We all know how to write a sentence, which communicates a thought. You wouldn't be reading this book if you didn't. But, there's much more you can learn.

Rhythm in dance comes from the arrangement of the steps choreographed to the beats of the music. Like dancing, each sentence has rhythm, fashioned from its length and composition.

We can string lots of words together to create a long, flowing sentence that takes many turns and twists and ultimately delivers the reader where he or she needs to be in a slow, easygoing manner, resembling a graceful waltz. Or we can jump right in. Use just a few words. Fill it with kicks and flicks. Dance a fast-paced jive.

Bite #163
How Much Is Enough?

Long, flowing sentences slow the reader's pace; short sentences quicken it. One is not better than the other. Sentences of all lengths are needed to hold the reader's attention.

Experts, whoever they are, disagree as to how many words make up the various sentence lengths. Some say short sentences contain up to fifteen or so words; medium sentences, from sixteen to twenty-five words; and long sentences, more than twenty-five words. I don't know about that. I've never been one to count words in my writing, but I do make a conscious effort to vary the lengths of my sentences.

I love this quote by Roy Peter Clark in his book, *Writing Tools: 50 Essential Strategies for Every Writer,* "Long sentences . . . create a flow that carries the reader down a stream of understanding. . . . A short sentence slams on the brakes." What you want the sentence to accomplish dictates its length and composition.

In his book *100 Ways to Improve Your Writing,* Gary Provost illustrates how varying sentence lengths enhances understanding and makes reading enjoyable:

> This sentence has five words. Here are five more words. Five-word sentences are fine. But several together become monotonous. Listen to what is happening. The writing is getting boring. The sound of it drones. It's like a stuck record. The ear demands some variety. Now listen. I vary the sentence length, and I create music. Music. The writing sings. It has a pleasant rhythm, a lilt, a harmony. I use short sentences. And I use sentences of medium length. And sometimes, when I am certain the reader is rested, I will engage him with a sentence of considerable length, a sentence that burns with energy and builds with all the impetus of a crescendo, the roll of the drums, the crash of the symbols—sounds that say listen to this, it is important.
>
> So write with a combination of short, medium, and long sentences. Create a sound that pleases the reader's ear. Don't just write words. Write music.

Bravo!

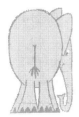

Bite #164
Not Just Fluff

When I was fourteen years old, I wanted to be a journalist. I convinced the editor of a local, weekly newspaper he didn't have enough news about the schools' activities, and he needed me to write a column. Somehow, he bought it, and "Teen Talk" was born.

I still have all those columns, and when I come across one every so often, I cringe. I thought I knew so much. The editor paid me twenty-five cents a column inch. Really, he didn't need to pay me; I would have paid him for the chance to see my name and words printed in the newspaper. Anyway, each month I cut out all my articles and literally took out a ruler and measured how many inches I wrote. That's how *stringers,* as opposed to *staffers,* were paid.

Math was *not* my subject, and I prayed my way through Mr. Aguillard's tenth-grade algebra class, but I didn't need to be a numbers whiz to figure out if I used ten words to say what I could in five, I'd get paid twice as much. I thought I was so clever. But those few extra pennies earned were not worth the habit I've struggled with ever since.

When I'm editing, I have to examine each sentence and take out the fluff. I look at each word to make sure it's necessary and contributing to the reader's understanding. If it isn't, down comes the ax. That word is history.

I encourage you to do the same. Maybe your sentences are too bare and need a little more detail and description. Go back to the Detail and Description section and find ways to color your sentences. Maybe your problem is like mine, and you need to delete words that don't contribute to the sentence. Maybe you're not quite sure what to do about sentences. That's okay. Just keep reading and writing.

Bite #165
Tighten Up

Sometimes we use more words than we need to because we think it sounds more important. Maybe we get this idea from legal papers, corporate letters and other documents from the business world. Certainly if we can't understand something, it must be significant, right? The answer is, no, not necessarily.

Writing that way does not work when telling your life story. The more you can write in a clear, concise, straightforward manner, the better your book will be. Let's look at a few examples where the delete key can be a star:

> He *is a man who* cares deeply for his children.
> He cares deeply for his children.

> This *is a* subject *that* is extremely difficult.
> This subject is extremely difficult.

He was sad *due to the fact that* he lost his job.
He was sad because he lost his job.

She feels better *at the present time.*
She feels better now.

I plan to see him *in the near future.*
I plan to see him soon.

When editing, take a look at your sentence and ask yourself a few questions: Do I need each word in this sentence? Is there a single word that could replace several words? Have I eliminated needless repetition? Give those sentences a workout, trim the fat and shape 'em up.

Bite #166
Run, Run, Run-On

We've learned about what makes up a sentence, what we can put into a sentence and what to do to vary a sentence. Now let's look at some of the things we *should not* do.

A run-on sentence is missing something—a conjunction or a semicolon. Here are a couple of examples:

Her father drove the wagon, her brother walked alongside.
Her father drove the wagon her brother walked alongside.

Here are a few things you can do to correct run-on sentences. You can break the sentence into two separate entities:

Her father drove the wagon. Her brother walked alongside.

Or you can connect the two parts with a conjunction or a semicolon:

Her father drove the wagon, and her brother walked alongside.
Her father drove the wagon; her brother walked alongside.

Problem solved. Case closed.

Bite #167
Fragmentville, Shades of Jimmy Buffet

The troublesome twin of the run-on sentence is a sentence fragment. Mr. Webster says a fragment is "an isolated, unfinished, or incomplete part," and that's what it is in writing. Like the run-on, a sentence fragment also has something missing—a subject or a verb—like these:

Drove the wagon. (No subject)
Her father and the wagon. (No verb)

To correct a sentence fragment, add what's missing, like so:

Her father drove the wagon. (Add subject)
Her father *drove* the wagon. (Add verb)

Bite #168
Leaves Me Wanting

Although only subjects and verbs are needed to create complete sentences, that doesn't mean *all* sentences containing those two items are good ones. The sentences might not technically be a fragment, but they still lack something to fully communicate the writer's meaning, such as:

Her father drove. (No object)

Her father drove . . . yes, it's a complete sentence, but *what* did her father drive? It could be a *hard bargain* or *a ball into the catcher's mitt* or *a wagon*. In this case, the meaning of the sentence is vastly different, depending upon object supplied.

Her father drove *the wagon.* (Add object)

That's better. I understand now.

Bite #169
Don't Dangle My Modifier

Way back at the beginning of this section, we talked about modifiers. Remember what they are? Of course you do: words that describe or qualify other words. Adjectives and adverbs are modifiers. Well, a phrase or clause can be a modifier, too, and the experts say it's *dangling* when it's in the wrong place or missing entirely. Let's look at the sentence we've been using:

Even though he was tired, her *father* drove the wagon.

The phrase or clause must be next to what it modifies. The clause, *even though he was tired,* modifies *her father,* so this sentence is correct. Here's a sentence that isn't so fortunate:

Even though he was tired, the *wagon* was loaded with vegetables.

What does *he* being tired have to do with the contents of the wagon? Absolutely nothing. The modifier needs to amplify the noun next to it. To correct this sentence, do one of the following:

Stacked high with crates and baskets, the *wagon* was loaded with vegetables.
Even though he was tired, her *father* drove the wagon loaded with vegetables.

The introductory phrases, *stacked high with crates and baskets* properly modifies the noun next to it, *the wagon,* and *even though he was tired,* modifies the noun, *her father.*

These dangling modifiers can be really funny at times. Look at some of these gems:

Covered with melted ice cream, we enjoyed our treat.

Covering yourself with ice cream—that's a different way to enjoy it. It sounds a bit chilly for my taste.

Dangling in the water, the *fish* nibbled on our toes.

Really, the fish were dangling in the water?

Flying over the Pacific Ocean, the *whales* breached before us.

Interesting. I didn't know whales could fly. Okay, I'm being silly, but I'm trying to make a point. If your modifier doesn't reside closely to what it modifies, you may end up with something funny or worse—embarrassment.

Punctuation

I will walk you through this required section as quickly and painlessly as possible. Granted, punctuation is not the most exciting topic in the world, and I know I risk putting you to sleep, but it is necessary. I'll do my best to keep us both awake.

As I said earlier, grammar and punctuation are only means to ends, not ends in themselves. Punctuation marks are best used like road signs. They tell us when to yield, pause or stop as well as provide many other directions designed to keep us on the road to our destination—a well-written life story.

This is not an exhaustive explanation of all those little marks sprinkled on the page. It is only a quick look. And know that for most stated rules about punctuation, you can easily find exceptions on the shelves of the nearest bookstore or on the pages of various style books. Here are some of the rules agreed upon by the *experts*.

Bite #170
Love Child—The Semicolon (;)

The other day I heard a semicolon called the *love child* of a colon and comma. Cute, but when should you use it? Three main uses exist for the semicolon: to connect two independent clauses, to join conjunctive adverbs (this sounds more complicated than it is) and to clarify a complex list.

The most common use of a semicolon is to connect two closely related, independent clauses without using connecting words like *and, or, nor, but, for, yet*. Remember, an independent clause is a complete sentence and can stand alone. In this example, the semicolon takes the place of the conjunction *and.*

> My grandmother loved soap operas, *and* she watched them every day.
> My grandmother loved soap operas; she watched them every day.

Secondly, semicolons are needed with conjunctive adverbs, those words that show comparisons, contrasts, cause and effect. They include words like *however, while, therefore, consequently, furthermore, nevertheless* and so forth. Use a semicolon to separate the two sentences and place a comma after the conjunctive adverb. Here's an example:

> My grandmother loved all soap operas; *however, General Hospital* was her favorite.

The third main use of the semicolon trips people up sometimes. It's used for clarity in a list that contains commas. Let me show you an example:

> My grandmother loved *Lee Baldwin,* a well-known lawyer; *Luke Spencer*; *Laura Webber,* Luke's wife; and *Dr. Steve Hardy.*

How many characters did my grandmother love? Correct, four people—Lee Baldwin, Luke Spenser, Laura Webber and Dr. Steve Hardy. You know that because the semicolons are grouping together the person and his/her description. What happens if only commas are used?

> My grandmother loved *Lee Baldwin,* a *well-known lawyer, Luke Spencer, Laura Webber,* Luke's wife, and *Dr. Steve Hardy.*

How many characters did my grandmother love? Correct, we've picked up two new people—Lee Baldwin, an un-named and well-known lawyer, Luke Spencer, Laura Webber, Luke's unidentified wife and Dr. Steve Hardy. In long lists, which include descriptive information, semicolons reduce confusion.

Bite #171
The Colon (:)

Colons separate minutes and hours when writing the time (*2:15 p.m.*); they are also used in salutations (*Dear Sir:*) and in citations (*Matthew 2:11*), but for our purposes, let's focus on the colon used to introduce a list. The colon replaces words which typically alert us to an upcoming list—*namely, for example, for instance.* Using a colon says, "Get ready. The second part of this sentence is going to explain or expand the first." No colon is needed if I write:

There are three ingredients that make *gumbo* great, *namely* onion, bell pepper and celery.

If I use a colon to introduce the list, it looks like this:

There are three ingredients that make *gumbo* great: onion, bell pepper and celery.

Bite #172
Make a Dash For It (—)

The dash is a great piece of punctuation and is created by putting *two* hyphens together; it's got to be two hyphens, not one. A single hyphen is just that, a hyphen. The dash is stronger than a comma and should be used in moderation. Any punctuation mark loses its effectiveness and becomes distracting if overused. Suddenly the reader is saying to herself, "There's that dash again," instead of paying attention to your words. Use it when needed, but don't get carried away.

The primary use for a dash is to indicate an abrupt change in a sentence:

She was his last thought—her blue eyes, wavy, brown hair and slight smile.

to set off explanatory information:

She was his last thought—her blue eyes, wavy, brown hair and slight smile—before he went to sleep each night.

or to designate a sudden break in a sentence:

She was his last thought—

Bite #173
Well, I Exclaim (!)

The exclamation mark is an overworked punctuation mark. Many writers force it to do the work they don't want to do or don't know how to do. Putting an exclamation mark at the end of a boring sentence doesn't make it exciting. Make your sentence exciting by choosing the right words, and you may not need the exclamation mark. And *never, never, never* use multiple exclamation marks to convince people this is *really* exciting. It won't make much difference to the reader, and it makes you look like an amateur. For example, I can write:

The rain is really coming down!

What does that mean? All rain comes down. Have you ever seen rain falling up? I'm being silly, but it's to prove a point. That little mark, which ends the sentence, is not strong enough to say much of anything. Instead, if I write:

The rain gushed from the dark, low-lying clouds surrounding us.

Does this sentence give you a better idea of how hard it is raining? I bet it does, and the exclamation mark isn't required.

I'm not prejudiced against the poor, little exclamation mark. When it's called for, use it, but don't wear it out. If you start putting exclamation marks at the end of every sentence, your reader isn't going to pay attention to them after the third or fourth one.

Bite #174
Comma, Man (,)

I saved the comma for last because few can agree on when to use or not use commas—not the style books, professors, writing instructors, high school teachers, grammarians, no one. Rarely has so small of a mark created such discussion and discord.

One client told me whenever a sentence is long, he figures it needs a comma somewhere, so he just throws one in. Unfortunately, I don't think his approach to using commas is all that unique. I have seen the little squiggle in some of the strangest places.

I am a traditionalist when it comes to commas, and I follow the rules of usage given by the old masters, so that is what I'll present here. But you don't have to look very far to find exceptions to what I say.

Until recently, I edited students' stories based on what E.B. White and William Strunk said in their classic, *The Elements of Style*, so I was constantly adding and deleting commas. Generally, if the comma usage is consistent, I leave it alone. That's the key word—*consistent*. You can't get creative with your comma placement and put it like this on one page and like that on another page. That makes it look like you don't know what you're doing. Pick a style of comma usage and stick with it throughout.

We've all been taught to put in a comma when we take a breath. Not so. A student in my class who taught English for more than thirty years once said, "We can't add in commas based on taking a breath because we all have different rates of respiration." I like that, and it's true. If we sprinkle our sentences with commas based on how we breathe, our stories can only be read properly by us.

With that said, the following comma bites may help.

Bite #175
Free to Be Me

Use a comma before conjunctions—*and, but, for, nor, yet, or, so*—connecting two independent clauses. Most of the grammar books agree on this one, but like I said, you can find many published memoirs where this rule is not followed. This is how the sentence should look:

> Grandma loved *General Hospital,* and she watched it every day.

Each half of this sentence can stand alone, so that makes it a sentence of two independent clauses joined by a conjunction; therefore, a comma should go before the *and.* If you choose not to use a comma in this situation—I certainly don't recommend it—but make sure you do it the same way on every sentence using this structure.

Bite #176
How Do You Do?

Use a comma to set off an introductory dependent clause. As you probably figured out, an introductory clause is one that introduces the main sentence or independent clause. It contains a subject and a verb, but its purpose is to enhance the main sentence. A comma is used to connect the two parts of such a sentence. It looks like this:

> After she thought about it for a while, Mom decided to make a big pot of chicken-sausage *gumbo* for the party.

Introductory clauses often begin with words such as *after, although, as, because, before, if, since, though, until, when* and so forth.

Bite #177
It's Just a Phase, I Mean Phrase

Use a comma to set off introductory phrases, words and expressions. Like the clause, an introductory phrase introduces the main sentence, but it does not have both a subject and a verb. A common type of introductory phrase is one that begins with a preposition. The English language has many prepositions—*about, after, at, before, by, for, from, in, into, on, onto, since, through, throughout, to, until, upon, with*, to name a few. Here's a sentence with an introductory prepositional phrase:

> In anticipation of the party, Mom cooked a big pot of chicken-sausage *gumbo*.

The same comma rule holds true when the introduction is only a word or two rather than a phrase:

> Yes, Mom is cooking a big pot of chicken-sausage *gumbo*. Tired or not, we will be there.

Many of the grammar books say if the introductory phrase contains fewer than six words, the comma isn't needed, but it's technically correct if you use it. I say use the comma all the time. It makes life much simpler.

Bite #178
Make a List

Use commas to separate items in a list. We already talked about the uses of semicolons in a complex list. Here we'll take a look at the commas that set off items in a series of three or more things. See the commas at work in this sentence:

> For the *gumbo*, Mom purchased a cut-up chicken, *andouille* sausage, onions, bell peppers, and celery.

The last comma before the *and* can be omitted. I came to life story writing from the journalistic side, and we never used a comma before the last item in a series, so that's the style I still use.

> For the *gumbo*, Mom purchased a cut-up chicken, *andouille* sausage, onions, bell peppers and celery.

Book publishers typically want that last comma. Pick your poison, but as I said earlier, be consistent in your choice.

Bite #179
So Descriptive

I talk about not overusing adjectives to describe a person, place or thing, but if you have to string a couple of adjectives together, separate them with a comma, like this:

> The rich, spicy broth of the *gumbo* warmed my soul.

This is what I *love* about grammar. You *always* separate the double adjectives with a comma *unless* it combines with another word to form a single adjective. Then you use a hyphen (long-stemmed roses). If the adjectives seem to be closely linked—typically those related to age, color, number, size or location—you don't use a comma or a hyphen (*ten short black dresses*). *Urrrrrrrrr.*

Bite #180
Use a Comma to Avoid Confusion

In the end, if the sentence has more than one meaning, or if the reader has to look over the text a second time to figure out the meaning, and a comma would help, put one in. For example:

Woman, without her, man would die.
Woman, without her man, would die.

Boy, what a difference. How opposite could the messages of these two sentences be? Commas can help you say what you mean.

Bite #181
To Comma or Not to Comma

Based on my years of teaching, I find people tend to use too many rather than too few commas. So, if you're not sure a comma is needed, it's probably not. Leave it out. You'll be correct the majority of the time.

Bite #182
Comma Splice

When I was learning to write in high school, I can't tell you how many times I saw *comma splice* written on my papers in red. I had a difficult time grasping the concept that a comma was not as powerful as I thought it was. Make sure you don't bump two independent clauses together without a semicolon or a conjunction. If you do, it's called a *comma splice*. A lowly, little comma is not enough to hold two mighty clauses together. Take a look:

Right: We listened to Cajun music; we danced the two-step.
Right: We listened to Cajun music, and we danced the two-step.
Wrong: We listened to Cajun music, we danced the two-step.

Okay, I'm done. I can only talk about commas for so long.

Bite #183
Parentheses ( )

What can I say about parentheses other than they are not my favorite punctuation marks? They are useful, and they do serve a worthwhile purpose. I guess it's more accurate to say I dislike the way they are used or overused. Some writers love parentheses (I'm not one of them), and every sentence (whether it needs it or not) includes parenthetical information (many times it's unnecessary).

The proper use of a pair of parentheses is to provide information to the reader that does not fit within the existing sentence structure. Usually it's *oh-by-the-way*, nonessential types of information. It's interesting but not really necessary to understand the point the author is making.

Parentheses distract the reader. Momentarily they move him or her from your main point to a secondary topic. If this is done too much, you risk losing your reader's attention.

My rule is to avoid using parentheses if at all possible. If you can't, use them sparingly. Save them for drawing all those happy and sad faces, :) or :(. Recently, I saw a cow someone drew primarily with parentheses, slashes, hyphens. That was fun.

```
        (__)
        (oo)
   /-------\/
  / |    ||
 * ||----||
   ~~    ~~
       Cow
```

Bite #184
Who Said That?—Quotation Marks

The most common use for quotation marks is to enclose words that are spoken in a story, more commonly known as dialogue. Single (' ') and double (" ") quotation marks serve different purposes. Let's discuss the double quotation marks first. Quotation marks set apart words attributed to a particular speaker. Use opening and closing quotes when you restate the exact words of the speaker.

Okay, I already can hear you, "There is no way I can remember the specific words spoken in a conversation from fifty years ago." Right, you cannot. Dialogue is *reconstructed* speech. Most of us can't remember the exact words from a discussion five minutes ago much less fifty years back. For now, set aside this concern, or go back and read the section on dialogue. Let's focus on the proper uses of quotation marks.

Quotation marks set off what is spoken from the rest of the words in a story, such as:

Mark asked, "Jill, would you like to go to the dance on Saturday night with me?"

Here we are using Mark's words to show him directly asking Jill to accompany him to the dance on Saturday night. This same sentence could be written as a paraphrased or an indirect statement where no quotation marks are necessary:

Mark asked Jill if she wanted to go to the dance with him on on Saturday night.

This is more of a statement of fact and not a recounting of what was actually said.

Bite #185
What's That Name Again? (" ")

The second major use of quotation marks is with titles of short works—chapters or individual stories within books, essays, short poems, short stories, songs, magazine articles, etc. The key word here is *short*. Place quotation marks around the titles of these kinds of works. (The titles of longer pieces like books, magazine and newspaper names, movies, plays, long poems—ones that are book length—television or radio programs, long musical works, etc., should be italicized, but we'll talk more about that a few elephant bites down the road.) Back to quotation marks. Here are a few examples:

> Did you read the poem "Hello, Hello Henry" by Maxine Kumin?
> I loved the article in today's paper titled, "Writing in the Rain."
> The song "New Attitude" by Patti LaBelle is one of my favorites.

Bite #186
All by Myself (' ')

Single quotation marks (' ') are used when someone is restating the words of another person who is not the speaker; in court this is called *hearsay*. Huh? This is really more difficult to describe than it is to do. Look at this example:

> Cliff said, "I heard Joyce say, 'I'm going to dress up as a gypsy' when she attends the Mardi Gras ball."

Here Cliff's statement is being quoted, and his words include the specific language used by Joyce. Does that help?

Single quotation marks set off secondhand speech. Period. That is the *only* use for single quotation marks. Some of my students must feel English grammar neglects single quotation marks because they use them in all sorts of ways. Nice thought, but it's incorrect. Only use them for quotes within quotes.

Bite #187
In or Out?

If you thought that last elephant bite was fun, wait until you read this. Where to put the standard sentence punctuation—inside or outside of the quotation marks—is subject to much debate by the experts and much confusion by those attempting to write their life stories. I will attempt to make it as simple as possible.

Put periods and commas inside the quotation marks. Put semicolons outside of the quotation marks. So far, so good, right? Put question marks and exclamation marks outside the closing quotation mark unless the question or exclamation marks belong within the quoted material. I told you this was going to be fun.

Enclosing periods and commas inside the quotation marks is accepted now. When my ninth-grade English teacher, Mrs. Gilbert, taught me about punctuation within quotations, it wasn't as straightforward as putting periods and commas inside the quotation marks, but now it is. Here are some examples:

> Joyce said, "I'm going to dress up as a gypsy for the Mardi Gras ball."
> Joyce asked Jolene to borrow her "fancy, gypsy costume," beads and hair ribbons for the Mardi Gras ball.

Semicolons typically fall outside of the end quotation marks, like so:

> Joyce said, "I'm going to dress up as a gypsy for the Mardi Gras ball"; she borrowed her costume from Jolene.

Moving on . . . question and exclamation marks. If the actual quote is a question, put the question mark on the inside of the ending quotation mark. If the entire sentence, not just the quote, is a question, put the question mark outside. Take a look as these examples:

> "Is John inside that dragon costume?" Joyce asked.
> "John, you look like a dragon!" Joyce exclaimed.
> Is the name of that song about a dragon "Puff the Magic Dragon"?
> Walking across the stage, John loudly sang "Puff the Magic Dragon"!

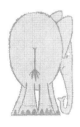

Bite #188
Leaning Letters—Italics

Italics resemble the Leaning Tower of Pisa; they look like they are going to topple over at any minute, but they won't. Italicize titles of newspapers, books, magazines, plays, movies, radio and television programs, works of art, long musical works, names of ships and airplanes, foreign words and to emphasize certain words. Again my mantra—use, but don't abuse the off balance, little letters.

> My mom read the *Times Picayune* from cover to cover.
> I loved James Lee Burke's book, *Purple Cane Road*.
> My ancestors arrived in Louisiana on the ship *L'Amitié.*

Bite #189
Who Made Up This Rule?

This is a rule that always makes me scratch my head. Even if a newspaper's complete, legal name is *The Franklin Banner Tribune,* we are instructed to *not* capitalize or italicize *the* and write it as follows: the *Franklin Banner Tribune*. I've never received a satisfactory answer as to why it's done that way. It is one of those *it's the way we've always done it* rules. So, it's not worth the fight. Just commit the rule to memory and "keep moving," like my husband says.

Bite #190
Long Gone

Before the days of computers with their easy ability to italicize text, we used quotation marks to set off words we wanted to emphasize and/or underlining to identify a title of a book or other major work. You don't have to do that today. Give a click to the little, slanted *I* on the toolbar of your word processing software and *voilà* . . . italicized letters.

It's not incorrect to use quotation marks or underlining in these instances, but it will let your reader know how old you are, that you're from the B.C. era, Before Computers, that is.

Bite #191
Hyphen Aid (-)

Use hyphens to write out numbers less than one hundred and fractions, like so:

My uncle caught *sixty-six* catfish.
His ice chest was *three-fourths* full.

If you string a few words together to describe something and the words are dependent on each other for meaning, use a hyphen to group them together, like this:

My uncle's fishing buddy was his *six-year-old* grandson Jason.
My uncle used a red and white bobber from his *well-stocked* tackle box.
My uncle's *son-in-law*, Cliff, is Jason's father.

To hyphenate or not to hyphenate, that is the question. Apply the *and* test here to determine if you need a hyphen or a comma to divide a preceding adjective. Separate each adjective with the word *and*. If the string doesn't make sense with the *and*, put in a hyphen. If the description reads okay, then use a comma; for example:

Six and year and old (It has to be six-year-old)
Well and stocked tackle box (It has to be well-stocked)

Bite #192
Super-Size It

We talked somewhat about capitalization in a previous section, but let me say a couple of more things here. When writing titles, you know to capitalize all the *big* words, all the important words. Sometimes, the important words can be little words, like *is*. Make sure you capitalize all verbs in titles, regardless of how many letters they contain.

The Tide Is Rising
I Am Who I Am

Always capitalize the first and last words in a title even if the last word is not normally uppercased.

What a Man Is Made Of
Where I'm From

Uppercase a title used to *signify rank, office* or *function* if it precedes a person's name or when the title is used in place of the name, but lowercase the title if it designates a position and not a specific person. Say what?

District Judge Robert Hebert or the *district court judge*
President Harry S. Truman or the *President* but *president* of the university
Reverend Joseph Landry or the *reverend* of the church

Okay, does that make it clear when we need to capitalize and when we don't? Try to remember it this way:

Title before the name—capitalize it
Title in place of a name—capitalize it
Title as a position—don't capitalize it

Bite #193
Big No-Nos

This breaks some people's hearts, but mostly, in life story writing there is no need for **bold text**, <u>underlined text</u> or TEXT IN ALL CAPS. None. It's different with academic and other types of writing, but for our purposes, remove the Caps Lock key and take the **B** and the <u>U</u> off your toolbar. You don't need them.

Bite #194
It Says To Do What?

Spelling and grammar checks built into word processing software packages are great tools and can alert you to misspellings, tense problems, sentence fragments, incorrect word choices, repeated words and many other common errors. But—and this is another big BUT—don't trust everything they say. They lie. Sometimes the advice given makes no sense. At other times, the system doesn't recognize a person's last name. My recommendation? Before making that change, check out the highlighted spelling or syntax problem in a grammar or style book.

Bite #195
Ask the Expert

Speaking of grammar or style books. . . . If you don't already have one, go out and buy one, right now. There are hundreds of books that purport to make grammar easy, painless or simple enough for a dummy. All of them contain valuable information that will help, if used. The key word in that sentence is *if.* You can have the best grammar book in the world sitting on your bookshelf, but if it's not cracked open, what good is it?

If you're crazy about grammar and punctuation and can't get enough of it, *The Chicago Manual of Style: The Essential Guide for Writers, Editors, and Publishers* is the book for you, all 1,026 pages of its sixteenth edition. There you can find more than you'd ever want to know about the written word, but it is not for the faint of heart. Finding what you need can be a challenge. *The Chicago Manual of Style* also has an online version, http://www.chicagomanualofstyle.org, which is available for an annual paid subscription.

For your most basic writing needs, I recommend the American classic, *The Elements of Style* by William Strunk, Jr. and E. B. White. Strunk penned the first version of this little book—currently fewer than a hundred pages—in 1918 as an easy-to-use guide for most writing questions, and White, who used the book as a student at Cornell under Strunk, revised it in 1957. The book is small, only 4½ by 7 inches, so you can put it in your pocket or bag and have it handy whenever you need to ask the expert.

Bite #196
A Word of Caution

A great deal of advice on grammar, punctuation and style can be found on the Internet as well, but not all of it is *good* advice. Check only the reputable sites for guidance. Many colleges and universities have online help available for anyone, not only students. One I use regularly is the Purdue University Online Writing Lab, OWL for short, which is located at http://owl.english.purdue.edu/. There you can find a wealth of basic writing information, and you can search the site for the proper way to handle a specific grammatical issue. And it's free!

Numbers

Math is not my strong suit. I write all numbers in my checkbook in pencil because I have a nasty habit of reversing the digits, but I'm a lot better with numbers in writing.

Consistency is the key when working with numbers in a story. You can find any number of *rules* about how to write numbers, and we'll go over a few of them, but whatever method you choose, be uniform throughout your story, and you'll be fine.

Bite #197
Numeral or Text

When using a number in our stories, the question is: "Do I use a numeral, or do I spell the number out in words?" The first two conventions surrounding numbers are ones most of the experts agree upon. They advise us to write out in words all numbers ten and under and use a word instead of a numeral to begin a sentence. After that, take your pick of the many options out there, but remember, you have to remain consistent in the path you choose to follow.

The Bible of writing rules, *The Chicago Manual of Style: The Essential Guide for Writers, Editors, and Publishers,* suggests we spell out "whole numbers from one through one hundred, round numbers, and any number beginning a sentence. For other numbers, numerals are used." Then it goes on for the rest of the chapter, talking about the *many* exceptions to that rule. Here are a few examples of the general rule:

I've gone to the Acadiana Festival of Music *twenty* times.
My grandparents' home is *two hundred* years old.
Sixty-three cousins showed up for Sunday dinner.
We had *1,412* students in our high school.

Here's one exception to the *spell-out-one-through-one hundred* rule. With really large numbers—the kind Stephen King makes from his book sales—you can use a combination of numbers and words, like so:

Simon paid *$3.5 million* for the rundown, plantation home.
Then he put another *$2 million* into it for renovations.
The Atchafalaya Basin formed *2.5 million* years ago.
More than *25 billion* atoms can fit on the head of a pin.

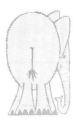

Bite #198
I Don't Do Math

Here are more general rules about numbers; hopefully, they won't overwhelm you. Okay, let's go.

Write out simple fractions.

She ate *three-quarters* of the pecan pie.
Two-thirds of the State rejected the amendment.

Use numerals for whole numbers plus fractions.

I walked *3¾* miles to get here.
My dad is 5 feet *8¼* inches tall.
Use *8½* x 11-inch paper for your story.

Always write percentages with numerals using the word *percent* or the symbol, %.

More than *80 percent* of family members came to the reunion.
She is *50%* French and *50%* Spanish.

With money, if words are used for the amount, then spell out *dollar* and *cents*.

A link of *boudin* used to cost *twenty-five cents.*

If you choose to use numerals with money, include the dollar ($) and cent (¢) signs. The cents sign is not on the standard keyboard. In MS Word, you have to insert it as a symbol.

I paid *$5* for that *Swamp People* cap.
Joseph saved his *25¢* to buy bubblegum.

Numbered street names usually follow the same guidelines as writing ordinary numbers—spell them out if one hundred or less; otherwise, use numerals.

First Street
Tenth Avenue
*131*st Street

Now that your head is swimming with numbers, care to look at time?

Bite #199
Got the Time?

If the time of day you want to use is a full, half or quarter hour, spell the number out. Any time you write out *o'clock,* the number has to be in words.

The *fais do-do* starts at *eight o'clock* and lasts until *eleven thirty* Saturday night.

Are you a morning or night person? Either way, you need to know how to write time correctly. Those little a.m. (ante meridiem) and p.m. (post meridiem) designations give people some trouble. If you use small caps, you don't need periods between the letters, but you need to know how to create them using your word processing software. That function is usually found on the font menu. Little caps look like this:

The *fais do-do* starts at 8:25 PM.

Without using small caps, it's best to use lowercase letters separated by periods such as this:

The *fais do-do* starts at 8:25 *p.m.*

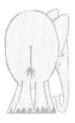

Bite #200
A Great Date

Writing dates can be a little tricky. I see quite a few mistakes made by students when fixing an event to a particular date. Express the year in numerals unless it's the beginning of the sentence. Here are a couple of examples:

My cousin James was born in *1954.*
Nineteen fifty-four was a good year to be born.

To shorten the year from four to two digits, use an apostrophe to represent the missing numbers:

My old high school held a reunion for the class of *'74.*

You just have to be sure your reader knows which century you are talking about. If I wrote '85, you wouldn't know if it should be 1685, 1785, 1885 or 1985, so make sure the context is clear when you substitute an apostrophe for the century.

This is a common error people make in writing dates. When writing about decades, you do not need an apostrophe to make the time span plural.

In the *1970s,* bell-bottom pants and mini-skirts were the rage.

An apostrophe used in this situation makes the decade possessive. Look at this:

I still have one of my *1970s'* mini-skirts.

Epilogue

Use as much or as little of this book as you desire. Sit down and read it all the way through, or pick it up only when you need it. Use it to turn an experience into a story. Use it as a reference when you have a question about punctuation or grammar or style. Use it as a guide to help bring to life a person who lives in your memory. Use it when you want to give the person a voice. Use it as a help to edit and revise your stories. Use it for encouragement, inspiration to keep you going. Use it in any way that benefits you and your writing, but make sure you use it.

I'd rather not visit you in a year and see *Eating an Elephant* in pristine, right-off-the-shelf condition, sitting on your coffee table. That's not the kind of book this is. Dog-ear it, underline and highlight phrases, write notes in the margins, spill coffee on it, bend it back, give it a workout. You—or someone who wants you to tell your story—paid for it, so get your money's worth out of every page.

Remember how we began this journey way back in bite number one? *The only way to do this wrong is to NOT do it at all!* If you try, you cannot fail, so pick up your pen or turn on your computer—yes, I mean right now—and write about the first thing that comes to your mind. Go!

Patricia Charpentier turned loss into passion when she embarked on a journey to help people give those they love the gift of a lifetime. She grew up in South Louisiana surrounded by extended family but had no desire to understand the history and culture she was born into. By the time she became interested, all those who held the answers to her questions were gone.

Through ghostwriting memoirs on behalf of others, as well as co-authoring, editing, teaching, speaking and publishing, Patricia has motivated and guided hundreds in leaving written legacies for their families.

Owner of Writing Your Life, a company devoted to personal and family history writing, and LifeStory Publishing, Patricia offers ongoing workshops and classes, including *online* classes, and is a popular speaker and seminar leader throughout Florida and South Louisiana. She lives in Orlando with her husband Bob.

Find out more about classes, workshops, presentations and how Patricia can help you write your life story at www.writingyourlife.org or contact her directly at writingyourlife@cfl.rr.com.

CPSIA information can be obtained at www.ICGtesting.com
Printed in the USA
241725LV00001B/9-154/P